The New Vic Theatre, Newcastle-under-Lyme presents

East Lynne

Adapted by Lisa Evans from the novel by Mrs Henry Wood

East Lynne

Adapted by Lisa Evans from the novel by Mrs Henry Wood

Company

Paul Barnhill	Archibald Carlyle
Justin Brett	Francis Levison
Juliette Goodman	Lady Isabel Vane
Maria Gough	Emma Vane / Joyce
Deborah McAndrew	Barbara Hare / Creditor
Alwyne Taylor	Cornelia Carlyle / Wilson / Mrs Crosby

Director	Gwenda Hughes
Designer	Lis Evans
Lighting Designer	Daniella Beattie
Sound Designer	James Earls-Davis
Company Stage Manager	Andy Billington
Deputy Stage Manager	Sue Yeomans
Assistant Stage Manager (on the book)	Imogen Ensoll
Music written and performed by	Sue Moffat

Set and props made by the New Vic Workshop.
Costumes by the New Vic Costume Department.

Lighting and sound operated by Daniella Beattie, Andy Kimberley, Phil Speck and James Earls-Davis.

The New Vic's production of *East Lynne* opened on Friday 24 June 2005.

There will be one interval of 20 minutes.

East Lynne

Adapted by Lisa Evans from the novel by Mrs Henry Wood

This adaptation of *East Lynne* was first performed on
16 December 1992 by Birmingham Repertory Theatre with
the following company:

Helen Baxendale	Lady Isabel Vane
Sean Cranitch	Archibald Carlyle
Chris Wright	Francis Levison
Janice McKenzie	Barbara Hare / Joyce / Emma Vane / Mrs Crosby
Lesley Nicol	Cornelia Carlyle / Wilson / Afy

Director	Gwenda Hughes
Designer	Kate Owen
Lighting Designer	Symon Harner
Company Manager	Sally Isern
Stage Manager	Karen Gow
Deputy Stage Manager	Richard Watson
Assistant Stage Manager	Diana Rowe

The New Vic Theatre

The Victoria Theatre Company was the first professional company in Britain to perform permanently in the round – that is, with the audience on all sides of the acting area. Today, the New Vic is known both for its professional productions and for its award-winning work in the community.

The company's origins go back to the late Stephen Joseph, director, actor, designer, lecturer and writer. In the late 1950s, along with other younger theatre practitioners, he was ambitious to renew the vitality of British theatre, founding the Studio Theatre Company to explore a new layout for performance: theatre-in-the-round.

The company's first base was Scarborough from which it toured the country taking the 'theatre' with it – raked platforms providing in-the-round seating for 250. Newcastle-under-Lyme was visited regularly and a permanent North Staffordshire home was planned. On 9 October 1962, a converted cinema opened its doors as a theatre, an event that received no mention in the national press. The company moved to a new, purpose-built theatre, The New Vic, in 1986.

Under the leadership of founding Director, Peter Cheeseman, the company became known for documentary drama with productions such as *The Fight For Shelton Bar* and *Jolly Potters* reflecting the preoccupations of and the issues affecting the communities of North Staffordshire, with its economy based on ceramics, coal and steel.

In 1998, Peter Cheeseman was succeeded as Artistic Director by Gwenda Hughes who has worked extensively in British theatre as an actor and director. For ten years, she was Associate Director with Birmingham Rep and has directed award-winning work in London's West End. Following her appointment, the New Vic has adopted an increasingly outward-looking and collaborative approach to the communities it serves, seeking to re-define the

Once We Were Mothers, September 2004
Photo: Northern Counties Photographers

Kitty And Kate, January 2005
Photo: Northern Counties Photographers

Two Days As A Tiger, TIE project March 2
Photo: The Sentinel

ways a theatre can contribute to the cultural, educational, social, recreational and economic life of the region.

This has led to the setting up of an Education Department to work within formal education, and the company's ground-breaking outreach department, New Vic *Borderlines*, which concentrates on work that encourages, enables and promotes Social Inclusion, Community Cohesion and Neighbourhood Renewal. Today, the Education and *Borderlines* departments are responsible for one third of the company's work.

Central to the company's ethos is the belief that each aspect of its work is of equal value. The language of 'audiences' has given way to one of 'engagement'. A young person devising a piece of theatre with *Borderlines*, the audience for a Shakespeare play, or a class of primary school children working on reading skills are all engaged with the New Vic and all are of equal importance.

The New Vic continues to address issues of concern to people locally. It believes in the power of theatre to change lives for the better. It believes that everyone has creative and artistic abilities and that, through encouragement, participation and example, they can be enabled to fulfil their creative potential.

The New Vic Theatre operates thanks to a unique partnership between Arts Council England, Staffordshire County Council, Newcastle-under-Lyme Borough Council and Stoke-on-Trent City Council

    Charity Number 253242

New Vic Theatre, Etruria Road, Newcastle-under-Lyme, Staffordshire, ST5 0JG
Administration: 01782 717954 Fax: 01782 712885 Box Office: 01782 717962 Website: www.newvictheatre.org.uk

The Company

PAUL BARNHILL ~ Archibald Carlyle
For the New Vic: *Kes, Romeo And Juliet*. At the New Vic (with Northern Broadsides): *The Merchant of Venice, Henry V, A Woman Killed With Kindness*. Theatre includes: *Twelfth Night* (Royal Shakespeare Company); *Whisper of Angels' Wings, Julius Ceasar, The Nativity, All That Trouble We Had* (Birmingham Rep); *Faustus* (Royal Theatre, Northampton); *Yeoman of the Guard* (Savoy Theatre); *Search and Destroy* (New End Theatre); *Anna Karenina* (Octagon Theatre, Bolton); *Death Of A Salesman* (Birmingham Repertory Theatre); *All's Well That Ends Well* (Nuffield Theatre, Southampton); *Taking Liberties* (Gateway Theatre, Chester); *Die Fledermaus* (Doyly Carte Opera Company); *Hamlet* (National Studio Theatre); *Tom Jones* (Theatr Clwyd & Tour). Television includes: *Doctors, Holby City, The Real Arnie Griffen, Anorak Of Fire* (BBC); *The Fabulous Bagel Boys* (BBC Scotland); *Brookside* (Mersey Television). Film includes: *Topsy Turvy* (Thin Man Films).

JUSTIN BRETT ~ Francis Levison
This is Justin's first appearance at the New Vic. Theatre includes: *The Real Thing* (Library Theatre, Manchester); *101 Dalmatians* (Gateway Theatre, Chester) *Blue/Orange, Strangers On a Train, Arms and the Man* (Theatre by the Lake, Keswick); *My Sister Sadie, This Is Where We Came In* (Stephen Joseph Theatre, Scarborough); *A Small Family Business* (West Yorkshire Playhouse); *Christmas On Mars* (Triple J Productions); *The Rivals* (Theatre Royal Bath); *Revenger's Tragedy* (Bridewell Theatre); *Deirdre Of The Sorrows, Revenger's Tragedy* (Riverside Studios); *Jinx, Clowns* (Orange Tree Theatre, Richmond); *The Shaughraun* (Gatehouse Theatre). Television includes: *Gory Greek Gods, EastEnders, Dombey & Son* (BBC); *The Bill* (Thames Television); *The Queen's Nose* (Film & General Productions); *London's Burning* (LWT); *Ghoul-Lashed* (Sky); *Dramarama* (Central). Film includes: *Randall's Flat* (Stage 2 Screen); *The Gothic Line* (Hit and Run Productions); *Brothers* (Brothers Films).

JULIETTE GOODMAN ~ Lady Isabel Vane
For the New Vic: *A Woman Of No Importance*. Theatre includes: The Settling Dust (Union Theatre, London); Popcorn - for which Juliette was nominated as Most Promising Newcomer in the 2004 Manchester Evening News Awards (Octagon Theatre, Bolton); *Private Lives* (York Theatre Royal); *No Way Out* (Soho Theatre); *A Voyage Around My Father, The Bus Ride* (Drayton Theatre); *Father And Sons, The Accrington Pals, She Would If She Could, A Month In The County* (Chanticleer Theatre); *Measure For Measure* (Extract for Shakespeare Garden Festival); *Eastward Ho!* (Greenwood Theatre); *Artist Descending A Staircase* (Arundel Festival). Television includes: *Max and Paddy* (Phil McIntyre). Juliette trained at the Webber Douglas Academy.

MARIA GOUGH ~ Emma Vane / Joyce

For the New Vic: *The Tenant Of Wildfell Hall, Moll Flanders, Who's Afraid Of Virginia Woolf*. Theatre includes: *Sailor Beware, Arms & The Man, Sleeping Beauty* (Theatre by the Lake); *Breaking The Code* (Sue Wilson); *Krindlekrax* (Birmingham Rep/ Nottingham Playhouse); *Love Me Slender* (Janice Chambers); *The Things We Do For Love* (Salisbury Playhouse); *Absurd Person Singular, The Tenant Of Wildfell Hall, The Winslow Boy* (Birmingham Rep); *June Moon* (Hampstead Theatre/ Vaudaville Theatre); *A Christmas Carol, The Nativity* (Octagon Theatre, Bolton); *Mrs Warrens Profession, Habeus Corpus, The Late Edwina Black* (Theatre By The Lake, Keswick/ Haymarket Theatre, Basingstoke); *Tis Pity She's A Whore* (Liverpool Everyman); *Romeo & Juliet* (York Theatre Royal). Television includes: *Booze Cruise, Emmerdale* (Yorkshire Television); *Coronation Street* (Granada); *Silent Witness* (BBC). Film includes: *In Memoriam* (Scorpions Screens).

DEBORAH McANDREW ~ Barbara Hare / Creditor

For the New Vic: *Pinocchio*. At the New Vic (with Northern Broadsides): *Much Ado About Nothing*. Theatre includes: *Sugar Sugar* (Bush Theatre); *Hard Times, The Malvern Widow, Her Big Chance* (Swan Theatre, Worcester); *A Midsummer Night's Dream, Anthony & Cleopatra, King Lear* (Northern Broadsides); *There's A Girl In My Soup* (Tour); *The Sound Of Music* (Queen's Theatre, Hornchurch); *Educating Rita* (Coliseum Theatre, Oldham); *Cabaret, The Rise And Fall Of Little Voice, Derby Day* (Octagon Theatre, Bolton); *Aladdin* (Pavilion Theatre, Rhyll); *Peter Pan* (Grand Theatre, Swansea); *Cinderella* (Grand Opera House, York); *Cinderella* (Connaught Theatre, Worthing). Television includes: *Coronation Street, A&E* (Granada); *Songs Of Praise, A Letter To Lilli, Holby City, This Is The Day* (BBC); *The Royal, Heartbeat* (Yorkshire). Radio includes: *The Spire, Wuthering Heights, The Red Balloon, A Half Name For A Half Person, Crazy Big Fish, The Blackpool Detective, The Soldier Moves, Fair Play, Lost empires, Heart & Soul, The Cinderella Service, The Distance Between Stars, My Sister's A World Class Kleptomaniac* (BBC). Deborah trained at Manchester University Department of Drama.

ALWYNE TAYLOR ~ Cornelia Carlyle / Wilson / Mrs Crosby

For the New Vic: *Pat And Margaret*. Theatre includes: *A Chorus Of Disapproval, The Revenger's Comedies, June Moon, The Linden Tree, Last Of The Red Hot Lovers* (Stephen Joseph Theatre, Scarborough); *Platonov, The Bed Before Yesterday* (The Almeida); *Trial By Jury* (Covent Garden Festival); *Three Sisters* (Bristol Old Vic); *The Nun, Spring Awakening* (Battersea Arts Centre); *Tess of the D'Urbervilles, Two, See How They Run* (Derby Playhouse); *The Norman Conquests* (Crucible Theatre, Sheffield); *Richard III* (Pleasance Theatre); *The Rover* (Salisbury Playhouse); *Swollen Tongues* (The Cochrane Theatre); *Once In A Lifetime, Company, Sweet Charity, Accrington Pals* (Library Theatre, Manchester); *Blithe Spirit* (Northcott Theatre, Exeter); *A Christmas Carol* (Liverpool Playhouse); *Abigail's Party, Top Girls* (Octagon Theatre, Bolton); *Piaf, Stepping Out , Home* (Coliseum Theatre, Oldham); *Gateway To Heaven* (The Oval); *A Small Family Business, David Copperfield* (West Yorkshire Playhouse). Television includes: *Midsomer Murders, Heartbeat, Casualty, EastEnders, Emmerdale, London's*

Burning, Devices and Desires, Strong Poison, Genghis Cohn (BBC Screen Two). Film includes: *The Old Curiosity Shop* (Disney); *Asylum* (Seven Arts Pictures). Radio includes: *The Outside Child, Diary Of A Provincial Lady, Bleeperman, The Golden Triangle* (Radio 4).

LISA EVANS ~ Writer

Lisa Evans' work for theatre includes: *Once We Were Mothers, Mother's Day, Vindication, Under Exposure* (British Theatre Association Award 1986), *Taking Liberties, Inside Out, Face Values, Stamping Shouting & Singing Home, Crime Of The Century, Better Than Burning* (South London Playwriting Award 1988), *The Red Chair* (British Theatre Association Award 1988), *Lucky Country, Christmas Without Herods, Slap, East Lynne, The Shadow Of Light, The Tenant Of Wildfell Hall, Getting To The Foot Of The Mountain* and *Jamaica Inn*. Her first play for radio was *Ring O'Roses*, followed by *Local Disaster, Aliens, Women Can Fly, Mary Seacole, Stamping Shouting & Singing Home, Hanging Fire* and *Laughter In Leningrad*. She also writes for television, work includes *Trainer, Casualty, Letting Go, Holby City, Peak Practice, The Bill* and *No Bananas*. She has been Writer in Residence at Theatre Centre, London and also for Temba Theatre Company. *Stamping Shouting & Singing Home* and *Under Exposure* are published in anthology by Methuen, and *Aliens* by Macmillan. *Once We Were Mothers, Getting To The Foot Of The Mountain* and *Jamaica Inn* are published by Oberon.

GWENDA HUGHES ~ Director

For The New Vic: *Dancing At Lughnasa, Pinocchio, Once We Were Mothers, A Woman Of No Importance, Four Nights In Knaresborough, Kes, Hector's House, The Beauty Queen Of Leenane, Romeo And Juliet, By Jeeves, Toad Of Toad Hall, Big Maggie, Who's Afraid Of Virginia Woolf?, Moll Flanders, The Wizard Of Oz, Office Suite, Broken Glass, She Knows You Know!, Othello, A Passionate Woman, The Tenant Of Wildfell Hall*. As Associate Director of Birmingham Rep over twenty-five productions including: *Whispers Of Angels' Wings, Landslide, The Winslow Boy, Nothing Compares To You, Loot, Entertaining Mr Sloane, Once On This Island* (also West End and Olivier Award for Best Musical), *Romeo And Juliet, Rope, Big Maggie, East Lynne, All My Sons, Translations, Noises Off* and *Hobson's Choice*; over fifty productions for children including, as Artistic Director of Watford Palace TIE, *Taking Liberties, Stamping, Shouting And Singing Home, Dirty Rascals, Flags And Bandages, Travelling Light, World's Apart* and *Past Caring* with adults and children with learning difficulties and, at Theatre Centre (London), *Billy The Kid, Inside Out, 1983, Face Values* and *Sack Of Lies*. Gwenda has worked as a freelance director with New Perspectives Theatre Company, Unicorn, M6, Red Ladder, Women's Theatre Group, The Young Vic, Oldham Coliseum, Lip Service, the National Youth Theatre and Salisbury Playhouse.

LIS EVANS ~ Designer

For the New Vic: As Resident Designer, over 60 productions including: *The Graduate, Kitty And Kate, Pinocchio, Stepping Out, Kes, My Night With Reg, The Lonesome West, The Beauty Queen Of Leenane, The Railway Children, By Jeeves, Cleo, Camping, Emmanuelle And Dick, Pat And Margaret, Toad Of Toad Hall, Top Girls, The Mikado, From A Jack To A King, Moll Flanders, The Wizard Of Oz, The Magic Flute, The Kiss Of The Spider Woman, Carmen, Translations, The Tempest, Aladdin, Return To The Forbidden Planet, Little Shop Of Horrors, Pirates Of Penzance, HMS Pinafore* and *Talking Heads*. Theatre - Design, painting and making for various productions in Nottingham, Manchester, Bradford, Edinburgh and London. Design Exhibitions - Cardiff, Stoke, Nottingham, Manchester, Sheffield and London. Lis trained at Cardiff Art School and Trent Polytechnic, Nottingham.

DANIELLA BEATTIE ~ Lighting Designer

For the New Vic: *The Graduate, Kitty And Kate, Pinocchio, To Kill A Mockingbird, Once We Were Mothers, Can't Pay Won't Pay, Amadeus, Beauty & The Beast, Kes, Carmen, Once A Catholic, The Lonesome West, Love Me Slender, The Duchess Of Malfi, The Marriage of Figaro, Outside Edge, The Beauty Queen Of Leenane, Pump Boys And Dinettes, Romeo And Juliet, Billy Liar, All That Trouble That We Had, Cleo, Camping, Emmanuelle And Dick, Pat And Margaret, Ham, Top Girls, Big Maggie*; co-design for *Who's Afraid Of Virginia Woolf?, Neville's Island, Office Suite*. For New Vic Borderlines and Education: *Our Country's Good, Blow The Whistle, Lost, The Caucasian Chalk Circle, The Ash Girl, Seasons Of Change, MC2, It's Just A Bit Of Fun, Inside Out, The Visit, A Midsummer Night's Dream, Home From The Past*. Other theatre includes: *The Mikado* (The Orange Tree, Richmond). Daniella graduated from Bretton Hall in 1995, joining the New Vic in 1997.

JAMES EARLS-DAVIS ~ Sound Designer

For the New Vic: all main house sound designs since 1987 including *The Graduate, Dancing At Lughnasa, Four Nights In Knaresborough, Carmen, The Lonesome West, The Duchess Of Malfi, Sweeney Todd, The Beauty Queen Of Leenane*. Original Music includes: *Once We Were Mothers, Kes, All That Trouble That We Had* (all with Russell Gregory), *Misery, Dealers Choice, Romeo And Juliet* (2001, with Sue Moffat), *Romeo And Juliet* (1996), *Broken Glass, Waiting For Godot, Dangerous Corner*. Sound Designs and /or Music for Borderlines and Education Projects includes: *Lost, Break The Silence, It's Not As Simple As Black And White* (all with Sue Moffatt), *Antigone, Our Country's Good, Jago's Box* (with Russell Gregory), *The Ash Girl* (with Ian Bayliss); *No Ball Games, Face It*. Production/Sound Editor for *Hitting Home, Radio Play* (by New Vic Borderlines in association with BBC Radio Stoke). Sound Design and /or Original Music includes: *Home Front, Sticks And Stones* (Reveal Theatre Co) *Twelfth Night* (Belgrade, Coventry), *Her Big Chance* (Harrogate), soundtracks for the films *On A Hiding To Nothing, A Good Earner?, Taken Without Consent, Dead Ball* (with Russell Gregory & Ian Bayliss) (Acting Out Company); several projects with Letting In The Light. Theatre - Sound Technician for the Redgrave Theatre, Farnham, Leeds Playhouse, Bristol Old Vic and Theatre School.

The New Vic Company

EAST LYNNE

First published in this adaptation in 2005 by Oberon Books Ltd
521 Caledonian Road, London N7 9RH
Tel: 020 7607 3637 / Fax: 020 7607 3629
e-mail: oberon.books@btconnect.com
www.oberonbooks.com

A catalogue record for this book is available from the British
Library.

ISBN: 1 84002 589 1

Cover image: *The Black Brunswicker* by John Everett Millais
© National Museums Liverpool

Characters

LADY ISABEL VANE

EMMA VANE, her cousin

CAPTAIN FRANCIS LEVISON

ARCHIBALD CARLYLE, the Vanes' lawyer

CORNELIA CARLYLE, his sister

BARBARA HARE, his neighbour

JOYCE, the Carlyles' maid

WILSON, the Hares' maid

AFY, Joyce's sister

MRS CROSBY

CREDITOR

VOICE OF WILLIAM VANE, Emma's son

VOICE OF (ISABEL) LUCY CARLYLE,
Isabel's daughter

VOICE OF LITTLE ARCHIE, Isabel's son

Note: This play can be performed by five actors (3F, 2M) by using the following doublings:

ISABEL

BARBARA / JOYCE / EMMA / MRS CROSBY

CORNELIA / CREDITOR / WILSON / AFY / VOICE OF WILLIAM /
VOICE OF LUCY

ARCHIBALD

LEVISON / VOICE OF ARCHIE

ACT ONE

Scene 1

ISABEL: Christmas. And the promise is made, whispered
in the dark across the fens and marshes, across the
rooves and gables. It is blown softly into the dreams of
wishful children, so they kick and fidget for morning.
This time it could happen. It could be true. A promise.
A promise. This time the child will be born and the
world made anew. There will be time for redemption.
So, blown along corridors, stirring dust in the attics of
memory, is the hope that echoes through all the pain of
childhood, of loss, of growing up. We shall be forgiven.
Beside the beds, kneeling, forgive us our trespasses as
we forgive them who trespass against us. And the child
is born with the voice in his heart saying I will die for
you. I will die for you.

Christmas. Snow falls, church bells ring joy to all
mankind. Victoria loves Albert and Albert loves
Victoria. All's well with the world. All children have fur
muffs and skate on frozen ponds that never crack, eat
chestnuts that never burn the fingers and always have
red rosy cheeks. Victoria loves Albert and Albert loves
Victoria. The family is certain. All's well with the world.

And because it is Christmas now, the time is come,
in the season of hope and redemption, to tell my tale
again. And this time I will tell it. And tell it true. For
there is a place, a place in the heart where even at
Christmas judgements are made without compassion
and there is no redemption. This place is cold and cruel
for it denies the warm blood of understanding and the
pulse of imagination. It judges and does not care. It
punishes and does not weep. The place is East Lynne.

Scene 2

A burst of cheerful music.

EMMA: May I introduce Lady Isabel Vane. Captain Francis Levison.

LEVISON: I'm enchanted. Merry Christmas to you Lady Isabel. It's so good to see a fresh face at these gatherings.

ISABEL: Is it? This is my first grand party.

EMMA: Isabel! Captain Levison will take you for a bumpkin.

ISABEL: Oh but I am. Doesn't it look just splendid? Everything sparkles. Just look at the frocks!

EMMA: Frocks!

ISABEL: Sorry, dresses.

EMMA: Frocks indeed. Isabel, you're not in the nursery now.

LEVISON: I expect your dance card is nearly full, Lady Isabel.

ISABEL: Oh no.

LEVISON: May I?

EMMA: Did your governess teach you nothing? You shouldn't let him see it, my dear.

ISABEL: Why not? It's quite empty.

LEVISON: Then I shall, with your permission put my name here and…

EMMA: Francis, you mustn't monopolise Lady Isabel, this is her first attempt at this sort of occasion.

LEVISON: If I don't monopolise you, someone else will.

EMMA: Captain Levison.

LEVISON: It always means trouble when cousin Emma calls me Captain. May I fetch you some fruit cup?

ISABEL: Thank you. That would be kind.

LEVISON moves.

Oh aren't the ladies' jewels splendid! So much finery.

EMMA: My dear, if I might offer a word of advice.

ISABEL: Have I done something wrong?

EMMA: No. No. But it does reflect upon our hostess. Especially in the festive season.

ISABEL: What does?

EMMA: Your dress. It's so plain. Almost as if you didn't care.

ISABEL: Oh but I do. I just didn't want to appear too fine. I did put on my diamonds but I took them off again. They seemed too showy.

EMMA: Yes, that necklace.

ISABEL: My mother gave me this cross.

EMMA: And it seems I am to bear it.

LEVISON approaches.

LEVISON: Here we are. Lady Isabel. Emma.

EMMA draws him aside.

EMMA: Thank you Francis. I shall be walking in the park tomorrow. I do hope you will be able to join me.

LEVISON: Tomorrow is another day, my dear Emma. I think the next is our dance, Lady Isabel? Lady Isabel?

ISABEL is trying not to cry.

The dance is beginning.

Would you rather sit this one out?

ISABEL glances at EMMA.

Some fresh air perhaps. The stars are beautiful tonight.

They move away from EMMA.

I find it hard to believe that you and Emma are related.

ISABEL: We're not. Well only by marriage. Her husband is my father's heir.

LEVISON: One always forgets Emma Vane has a husband.

Beat.

What did she say to you?

ISABEL: I don't know what you mean.

LEVISON: You mustn't mind her. She's only jealous.

ISABEL: No. I'm foolish to care.

LEVISON: To let her barbs hurt you, that is foolish. But to care? No. Caring requires courage.

ISABEL: I'd like to be brave.

LEVISON: Then come and dance with me. That requires a deal of bravery, I assure you.

ISABEL: Are you such a bad dancer?

LEVISON: On the contrary. I think I'm so frightfully good I'm bound to come a cropper and bring you crashing down with me. Do you care to risk it?

ISABEL: (*Laughing.*) Are you always so silly?

LEVISON: I didn't want you to cry.

They start to waltz.

ISABEL: That was kind of you.

LEVISON: Careful, you'll ruin my reputation.

ISABEL: What's that?

LEVISON: You mean you haven't heard?

ISABEL: I've not been much out in society. There's only my father and me, you see, and he's not very well.

LEVISON: I am sorry.

ISABEL: Should I ask him about your reputation?

LEVISON: Oh no. I wouldn't go as far as that. I'll confess it freely. You see I'm a single man in line for a title one day and I won't marry any of their daughters.

ISABEL: Whose?

LEVISON: (*Gesturing round the room.*) Theirs.

ISABEL: Why not?

LEVISON: I have no money. So that automatically gives me a bad reputation. Which I strive to maintain, for my own protection. Some of these mamas have a grip like a bulldog. Lady Isabel, you're not taking me seriously.

ISABEL: Indeed I am not. I think you are just trying to shock me. Talking of marriage like that.

LEVISON: I see. But what about my dancing? What do you think to that?

ISABEL: Well, we haven't fallen yet.

LEVISON: And will you be spending the rest of the season here in town?

ISABEL: No, my father and I are going to East Lynne for Christmas.

LEVISON: I've heard his estate is a beautiful place.

ISABEL: I can only just remember it. We left when I was still a child, after my mother died.

LEVISON: Will that not be sad for you?

ISABEL: Oh no, my parents were very happy there. I want to go to East Lynne.

LEVISON: They'll all come out to look at you. The whole town of West Lynne will want to see Lady Isabel Vane return. Is she still climbing trees and falling into brooks?

ISABEL: Certainly not. How did you know?

LEVISON: I didn't. Till just now.

ISABEL: But you know West Lynne?

LEVISON: I passed through once. I remember it as a very important place, in its own eyes. I didn't stay long. The dance is over.

ISABEL: (*Disappointed.*) Oh.

LEVISON: We'll meet again. Good luck at East Lynne!

LEVISON exits.

Scene 3

Montage as ISABEL is greeted by one after another of the luminaries of West and East Lynne.

BARBARA: Welcome to East Lynne, Lady Isabel.

ARCHIBALD: Lady Isabel, may I introduce myself? Archibald Carlyle. I came to see your father some time back.

ISABEL: Pleased to meet you.

ARCHIBALD: You were out dancing I believe. Archibald Carlyle. At your service.

ISABEL: Thank you.

BARBARA: Miss Barbara Hare. We live at The Grove. We're neighbours.

ISABEL: Oh yes, how kind.

BARBARA: Barbara Hare. I called before and left my card.

ISABEL: My father has not been well.

BARBARA: How sad. What a homecoming.

ISABEL is handed a pile of calling cards and invitations by the performer playing JOYCE.

ISABEL: At home. At home. Mrs Dobede. Justice and Mrs Hare, The Grove.

WILSON: Wilson milady, Miss Barbara's maid. A word.

ISABEL: Of course. Miss Barbara?

WILSON: Miss Barbara Hare. At home.

ISABEL: Peter! The carriage. I must leave my cards.

ISABEL reads more cards.

Miss Cornelia Carlyle. Mr Kane. A concert. The Misses Dobede. Tea dance. At home. At home. Archibald Carlyle. Mr Carlyle, my father will see you now.

ARCHIBALD: You've not met my sister Cornelia.

ISABEL: How do you do?

CORNELIA: I saw you after church, Lady Isabel. Climbing into a very fine carriage.

ISABEL: Why yes, thank you.

CORNELIA: I always walk.

ISABEL: Do you? Will you take tea?

CORNELIA: Better for the soul. And the constitution.

ISABEL: Or something stronger.

ARCHIBALD: I'm sorry your father's gout is worse.

CORNELIA: I never drink.

ISABEL: Thank you for coming. A glass of wine?

CORNELIA: My brother never drinks.

ARCHIBALD: I don't mind if I do.

JOYCE: So sorry for interrupting. I'm Joyce Hallijohn milady. I just come to retrieve Miss Corny's bonnet.

ISABEL: Not at all. Joyce Hallijohn.

JOYCE: Yes, upper servant at the Carlyles'. In West Lynne.

ISABEL: Joyce Hallijohn. What a nice name.

JOYCE: Thank you milady. Hope you'll be happy.

ARCHIBALD: To see your father, Lord Mount Severn?

ISABEL: He's not well. The doctor…

ARCHIBALD: Don't you worry.

ISABEL: Is he in pain? No one will tell me.

ARCHIBALD: If I can be of service.

BARBARA: Barbara Hare.

ARCHIBALD: At any time.

CORNELIA: Cornelia Carlyle.

BARBARA: My card.

ARCHIBALD: Any time at all.

CORNELIA: My card.

BARBARA: Your neighbour.

ARCHIBALD: Lawyer.

CORNELIA: Brother.

JOYCE: Servant.

ARCHIBALD: Friend.

This scene has whirled to a crescendo.

ISABEL: Father? Father! No!

Scene 4

ARCHIBALD and ISABEL are together on stage.

ARCHIBALD: Now calm down Lady Isabel and speak clearly. Who are all those people in the hall?

ISABEL: Creditors, Mr Carlyle. It seems my father, the late Earl Mount Severn, owes money to half the country. I never knew. He never told me.

ARCHIBALD: Now then, calm. Calm. No point in getting hysterical.

ISABEL: There is no money to pay anybody, even to buy food for the servants' breakfast. Everywhere I go in my house people accost me for money they are owed. My father is dead. And there are two men upstairs in my father's room standing guard over his body.

ARCHIBALD: The undertakers?

ISABEL: They won't let the undertakers in. Dear God, they won't let him go. My father!

ARCHIBALD: Who won't?

ISABEL: They say – They say they've taken possession of him.

ARCHIBALD: Taken possession...!

ISABEL: Of, of his body. They say the coffin won't be leaded and nailed down till they're paid what they're owed. I don't have any money. There is no money. I don't know what to do.

ARCHIBALD: It's obscene. And in this heat too. I'm sorry. And all those people in the hallway. They want money too?

ISABEL nods.

I better talk to them first.

ARCHIBALD goes to call off, hesitates.

With your permission, Lady Isabel.

ISABEL nods.

(*Calling.*) Send in one of your number. I'll not deal with a multitude.

(*To ISABEL.*) Don't worry, I'll handle this.

A woman CREDITOR enters.

CREDITOR: It's not good enough. He's ruined thousands and yet his daughter hasn't even the courage to come down and speak to us.

ARCHIBALD: She is here now. But I am acting for her. Kindly address your complaints to me.

CREDITOR: He bought the goods, now he must pay for them. That's the law. If my boy were to steal so much as a turnip he'd be beaten or sent to prison.

ARCHIBALD: I understand how you feel…

CREDITOR: Well where does that leave us? We want our debts paid.

ARCHIBALD: You must go to the late Earl's solicitors. Curzon and Guyett I believe.

CREDITOR: Oh we've been there. Nothing doing.

ARCHIBALD: At any rate you'll get nothing here. Please I must ask you again to leave the house at once.

CREDITOR: Who are you to tell us to leave?

ARCHIBALD: For one thing, you're trespassing on private property.

CREDITOR: Well the Earl's not going to mind that now, is he?

ARCHIBALD: East Lynne no longer belonged to the Earl when he died.

CREDITOR: What d'you mean?

ARCHIBALD: Earl Mount Severn sold the property in its entirety some six months ago.

CREDITOR: What, furniture and everything?

ARCHIBALD: Everything.

CREDITOR: That's not right. If he had money we should have been paid then!

ARCHIBALD: That's as maybe.

CREDITOR: Who says he sold East Lynne?

ARCHIBALD: I do.

CREDITOR: And who are you?

ARCHIBALD: Archibald Carlyle. Lawyer and advocate.

CREDITOR: Yes well, how do I know you're not making this up to get rid of us?

ARCHIBALD: Because Earl Mount Severn sold East Lynne to me.

ISABEL: To you?

CREDITOR: What, and carried on living here? It's a fiddle.

ARCHIBALD: The Earl was staying here as my guest until his health recovered.

CREDITOR: That did he do with the money then?

ARCHIBALD: I have no idea. And now I would ask you to leave my house.

ISABEL: Maam. I'm so very sorry. I didn't know anything of all this. Believe me. My father never told me how things were. I believe I have nothing but if I had, it would belong to you.

CREDITOR: Yes, it would. It damn well would.

ARCHIBALD: Please, go now. Don't make me use the law.

CREDITOR: Law! We're the one's been robbed. Law should be on our side.

ARCHIBALD: Nevertheless, the position is…

CREDITOR: The law's on the side of them with money. I know.

ISABEL: I promise you, I knew nothing of this.

CREDITOR: Keep your promises. You'll need them to live on. Good luck to you.

The CREDITOR exits.

ARCHIBALD: I'm so very sorry you had to go through that, Lady Isabel.

ISABEL: You own our house. East Lynne is yours?

ARCHIBALD: Yes.

ISABEL: Since when?

ARCHIBALD: Since last June. Your father never told you?

ISABEL: No. Never. And neither did you, Mr Carlyle.

ARCHIBALD: It was not my place.

ISABEL: All this time you've been coming here, watching us, knowing. How could you!

ARCHIBALD: Your father wanted it kept a secret.

ISABEL: Why should he?

ARCHIBALD: You saw those people. They are but the first of many.

ISABEL: How you must have laughed at me, calling this home.

ARCHIBALD: I understand you are upset. But I bought the property, fairly and legally from the late Earl Mount Severn. I think I can understand your distress but – forgive me – you are very young, and the secrecy was none of my doing.

ISABEL: And all these things, linen, cutlery, do they belong to you?

ARCHIBALD: I believe they're now your cousin's, the new Earl Mount Severn. Along with the jewellery and the pictures.

ISABEL: Candelabra, curtains, rugs, books, pots, pans?

ARCHIBALD: There is an inventory.

ISABEL: Are my clothes my own?

ARCHIBALD: I'm sure they are.

ISABEL: Would you be so kind as to consult your inventory just to make sure. I need to know, you see. The world has turned upside down and I cannot act if I do not know the truth of my situation.

ARCHIBALD: They are yours.

ISABEL: Perhaps you could tell me when you would like me to leave your house.

ARCHIBALD: Whenever it is convenient to you. Where will you go?

ISABEL: I don't know. There was only my father and me.

ARCHIBALD: I am sure your cousin will be happy to give you a home.

ISABEL: Live with Emma Vane? She hates me. I can't go there.

ARCHIBALD: I will see to those men upstairs.

ISABEL: Thank you.

ARCHIBALD: Lady Isabel?

ISABEL: What?

ARCHIBALD takes her hand.

ARCHIBALD: I am truly sorry for your loss. I will do anything I can to be of service to you now, or at any time in the future when you may wish to call on me.

ISABEL: Thank you Mr Carlyle.

ARCHIBALD leaves. ISABEL looks down at her hand.

Mr Carlyle...

She unfolds a bank note.

One hundred pounds.

She scrumples it up. She can't afford to do this. She wants to give it back. She can't afford to. She smoothes it out again.

Thank you.

Scene 5

ISABEL is sitting and mending a child's kite. EMMA bustles in.

EMMA: Ah there you are Isabel. I wondered where you were hiding.

ISABEL: I wasn't hiding.

EMMA: Well whatever you like to call it. I'm sure my guests are always remarking on how you sulk in corners. As if you were a guilty housemaid, one said.

ISABEL: Have you lost something?

EMMA: Yes, my garnet brooch. I swear I was wearing it earlier.

ISABEL: Maybe it fell off.

EMMA: And maybe it just walked away on little legs. Ah well. These things happen. If you should come across it, please return it to my maid. I'll quite understand. As long as it comes back soon.

Well, I'm going out for a drive. With Lieutenant Mouncey. Once he'd prised himself away from your grasp at yesterday's soirée he confessed he'd never seen the water meadows at Castle Marling. So I am to be his guide.

ISABEL: How nice.

EMMA: Well, I'll have an opportunity to get a word in edgeways won't I? By the way, Mrs Pinnock is calling with a sample of a new paisley I want her to make up for me. If I'm detained you can entertain her can't you?

ISABEL: Very well.

EMMA: We must get her to run you up something new as well, mustn't we? Can't have you looking dowdy. Now I understand the anxiety mothers feel at having daughters perched on their shelves. Thank goodness I have only boys.

ISABEL: Emma.

EMMA: Lady Mount Severn in the drawing room.

ISABEL: Lady Mount Severn. I understood you to imply I talked too much to your male guests yesterday.

EMMA: I never said any such thing.

ISABEL: And now I am an unmarried burden on your household.

EMMA: Why, you are a sensitive little flower today.

ISABEL: Perhaps I should talk to your husband and consider taking a position as a governess somewhere.

EMMA: What, and have the world say I turned you out of doors? A Lord's daughter? Don't be so silly.

ISABEL: I'm not here of my own choice.

EMMA: Nor of mine. Why don't you take a turn in the garden? Get some fresh air. You look like a plate of nursery food.

EMMA leaves.

ISABEL looks in her purse and counts what money she has left. It's not enough. We hear the voice of WILLIAM – EMMA VANE's small son.

ISABEL puts down the kite and responds to it as if it were WILLIAM.

WILLIAM: Is it mended?

ISABEL: Oh William, you startled me.

WILLIAM: My kite. Is it mended?

ISABEL: Yes, I think so.

WILLIAM: Were you planning on running away?

ISABEL: No. No, not really.

WILLIAM: Mama had my pocket money stopped too.

ISABEL: Oh dear.

WILLIAM: Yes. For answering back. All I said was I'd
rather look after pigs than go to Eton.

ISABEL: Why was that answering back?

WILLIAM: You know how grown ups are.

ISABEL: Yes.

WILLIAM: Shall we fly the kite?

*ISABEL laughing, swirls the kite round. WILLIAM giggles
with delight.*

Scene 6

*LEVISON enters and joins ISABEL. They and WILLIAM
have all been out walking.*

*WILLIAM is again a voice and the kite which ISABEL places
on the stage and which is talked to as if to the child.*

LEVISON: Tramping the fields has brought the colour to
her cheeks, eh William?

WILLIAM: She's my favourite person. Except Mama and
Papa of course. And Growler and farmer Manson's new
piglets.

ISABEL: Why thank you. I'm honoured.

WILLIAM: You like her too don't you Francis?

LEVISON: Of course. Everyone likes Lady Isabel.

ISABEL: Weren't the bluebells just so...so...

LEVISON: She's run out of words at last Will.

WILLIAM: No she hasn't. Come on Isabel.

ISABEL: They were just so...

LEVISON: Blue?

ISABEL laughs.

WILLIAM: Sniffy?

ISABEL: No. Hopeful.

LEVISON: She's been reading poetry again Will.

WILLIAM: I like poetry. It rhymes.

ISABEL: There you are you see, all boys don't have to be philistines.

WILLIAM: The Philistines be upon thee Samson!

LEVISON: What?

WILLIAM: The Philistines be upon thee Samson!

ISABEL: It's from the Bible Captain Levison.

WILLIAM: Yes, the bit about haircuts.

LEVISON: I see.

ISABEL and WILLIAM laugh at LEVISON.

Another hole in my education.

ISABEL: William, your mother will be wondering where you've been all afternoon.

WILLIAM: No she won't. She's entertaining.

LEVISON: There was no company here when we left. How do you know?

WILLIAM: She was pinching her cheeks and putting black on her eyes.

LEVISON: See how observant we philistines are, Lady Isabel.

EMMA enters.

WILLIAM: Oh Isabel doesn't wear paint. She doesn't need to.

ISABEL: William dear you forget yourself.

EMMA: He is not alone. Francis, I thought you were otherwise engaged this afternoon?

LEVISON: I was. But I cried off. It was such a beautiful day.

EMMA: Really.

LEVISON: But now it appears to be clouding over. I think I'll make my retreat. Goodbye Lady Isabel. Remember, all storms pass. William, another day I'll race you and win. Emma.

EMMA: Good day, Captain Levison.

LEVISON exchanges a look with ISABEL and beats a hasty retreat.

And where have you been all this time?

ISABEL: Out walking.

WILLIAM: We saw piglets – lots of them.

EMMA: Be quiet William.

WILLIAM: I love piglets.

EMMA: Don't be disgusting. So, this is the way you chose to repay my hospitality is it?

ISABEL: I don't know what you mean.

EMMA: Don't play the innocent with me. Three hours you've been hiding in the bushes with Francis Levison.

WILLIAM: We didn't go in any bushes. We went to see the piglets –

EMMA: William, be quiet.

WILLIAM: And the bluebells.

ISABEL: I assure you I've done nothing to be ashamed of.

EMMA: Is that so? Not from where I stand. You've been flirting with him from the moment you arrived. You did nothing else at Christmas. I've never been so embarrassed in my life.

ISABEL: You had no cause. I do not flirt. I have never flirted.

EMMA: It's the desperation that's so pathetic.

ISABEL: There is only one person in this house who flirts and that's you Lady Mount Severn. And not with your husband!

EMMA slaps ISABEL hard.

WILLIAM: (*Wails.*) Mama?

EMMA boxes WILLIAM's ears. He wails. EMMA sweeps out, taking the kite with her. ISABEL cries.

ISABEL: Oh get me out of this, please God, get me out of this.

ARCHIBALD enters.

ARCHIBALD: Excuse me.

ISABEL quickly composes herself.

Lady Isabel. Please excuse me.

ISABEL: Mr Carlyle!

ARCHIBALD: I had business in the town. I couldn't leave without calling on you.

ISABEL: As you see. I'm still here.

ARCHIBALD: And you are well I hope.

ISABEL: Very well, thank you. And you?

ARCHIBALD: Oh, fair to middling. As always.

ISABEL: And your sister, Miss Carlyle?

ARCHIBALD: Cornelia is fighting fit. As always. What lovely weather we're having. Most clement.

ISABEL: Indeed.

ARCHIBALD: We've had some terrible rainstorms.

ISABEL: Oh dear. Have you?

ARCHIBALD: Yes. Flooded the cellars of the butchers.

ISABEL: How dreadful.

ARCHIBALD: Yes. Not good for business. Rain. Stops people buying things.

ISABEL: But good for the flowers.

ARCHIBALD: Oh. Flowers. You should see the flowers at East Lynne. Carpets of bluebells, daffodils. People still ask after you there. But I expect you're happy to be here amongst your family.

ISABEL breaks down.

What did I say? Oh Lady Isabel. Forgive me. What was it?

ISABEL: Mr Carlyle, you said nothing untoward. It was not your fault.

ARCHIBALD: But then…

ISABEL: I am not happy here.

ARCHIBALD: But –

ISABEL: Tell me about East Lynne. Have you tenants for it?

ARCHIBALD: Not yet. I know East Lynne was a sad place for you but things seem to have got even worse for you since then.

ISABEL: East Lynne sad? Oh no. I dream of going back there and father alive. It was my home for the first seven years of my life. Oh no, I was happy there.

ARCHIBALD: And could be again!

ISABEL: I'm sorry?

ARCHIBALD: You could return, as its mistress.

ISABEL: I don't see how that could be. It's only a dream.

ARCHIBALD: Not if you were to become my wife.

ARCHIBALD sinks to his knees.

ISABEL: Please Mr Carlyle get up.

ARCHIBALD: I would do my utmost to make you happy. East Lynne would be yours. You would be free to rule in your own home. Mistress of East Lynne.

EMMA enters to find ARCHIBALD on his knees before ISABEL.

EMMA: Good afternoon.

ARCHIBALD: (*Rising.*) Archibald Carlyle.

ISABEL: Lady Mount Severn.

ARCHIBALD: I am acquainted with your husband milady. And a friend of the family.

EMMA: So I see.

ISABEL: Let me explain.

EMMA: Quite an extraordinarily intimate scene to come upon in one's drawing room. Whatever will you come up with next, Isabel?

ARCHIBALD: I was asking Lady Isabel to grant me the honour of becoming my wife.

EMMA: Your wife!

ARCHIBALD: And to come and be mistress of East Lynne.

EMMA: Why how perfectly wonderful. What a good idea. I hope you said yes, my dear?

ISABEL: I am taken by surprise. I would like some time to think.

EMMA: Don't take too long.

ARCHIBALD: You've given me hope.

EMMA: We'll leave you to think. Think hard Isabel.

EMMA and ARCHIBALD exit.

ISABEL is alone with her thoughts.

She looks up to see LEVISON has entered.

ISABEL: Captain Levison. You startled me. It was as if I thought you and then you were there.

LEVISON: Powerful thoughts. I've just heard your good news.

ISABEL: Good news?

LEVISON: Why, of your engagement to Mr Carlyle. He seems a good sort of a fellow. I hope you'll be happy.

ISABEL: I haven't said yes.

LEVISON: East Lynne is a catch in itself.

ISABEL: I don't want a catch.

LEVISON: Oh?

ISABEL: (*She can't say she wants him.*) I can't stay here any longer.

LEVISON: Then your only way out is marriage.

ISABEL: You would approve of my accepting Mr Carlyle?

LEVISON: What choice do you have my dear? I wish I…

ISABEL: Yes?

LEVISON: Best to say I'm not the marrying kind. I wish I were.

ISABEL: I shouldn't be talking to you like this.

LEVISON: No. It is not at all proper.

ISABEL: I have no one else.

LEVISON: I can't help you Isabel. I have nothing to offer you.

ISABEL: Forgive me for being so foolish as to imagine…

LEVISON: Be happy. Strive to be so and it will happen. Good luck.

LEVISON leaves.

ISABEL recovers herself then calls out.

ISABEL: Mr Carlyle! What choice do I have?

Scene 7

A peel of wedding bells. ARCHIBALD enters, kisses her, whirls her round.

ARCHIBALD: Mrs Carlyle. Welcome to East Lynne.

CORNELIA enters.

Cornelia! You here, how kind of you. Isabel, you remember my sister.

CORNELIA: How d'you do Maam.

ISABEL: Oh please call me Isabel.

CORNELIA: I'll try to remember.

ARCHIBALD: It's good to be home. The inn we stayed at last night was, well…

ISABEL and ARCHIBALD share a private joke.

…somewhat cramped.

CORNELIA: I've ordered breakfast. Come through. After you Maam.

ARCHIBALD: You must have been up with the lark this morning Cornelia, to come all the way from West Lynne to organise this.

CORNELIA: It's no problem.

ARCHIBALD: Well we're very grateful. I had been just a little afraid that you might be cross with me, Corny.

CORNELIA: Why ever should I be?

ARCHIBALD: Surprising you with my good news.

CORNELIA: Oh you mean letting me, your only sister who brought you up, know of your marriage after the event and by letter, oh no, why should I be cross?

ARCHIBALD: Your bark always was worse than your bite. You'll see, Isabel. Where are the servants? They should have been here to greet their new mistress.

CORNELIA: Oh I sent them away.

ARCHIBALD: What?

CORNELIA: The money you must have wasted on those fancy uniforms. Such airs. It never would have worked, Archie.

ARCHIBALD: But I employed them.

CORNELIA: And I dismissed them.

ARCHIBALD: But Cornelia…

CORNELIA: We can manage fine with Joyce and the other two servants we are used to.

ARCHIBALD: We?

CORNELIA: Yes, I've moved in.

ISABEL: Moved in here?

CORNELIA: I saw no point in the expense of running two establishments for one family.

ISABEL: Here?

CORNELIA: Archibald's all the family I've got you see Maam. I raised him when our mother died.

ISABEL: You must be very fond of him.

CORNELIA: So that's settled then. (*Catching a look from ISABEL to ARCHIBALD.*) Unless of course the arrangement doesn't suit you Maam.

ISABEL: No no indeed.

ARCHIBALD: What about your own house?

CORNELIA: I've let it. So I've no home to go to. You'll understand how that feels, Lady Isabel.

ARCHIBALD: Isabel has come home. To East Lynne.

CORNELIA: Well, I daresay I'll be very useful to her as a housekeeper. I think you'll find I earn my keep.

ISABEL: Oh I never meant to imply...

ARCHIBALD: Leave it to me Isabel. You're tired. After the journey.

ISABEL: I was only going to say... That I'll be very pleased to have you here Miss Carlyle.

ARCHIBALD: Cornelia.

ISABEL: Cornelia.

CORNELIA: Maam. Would you like to see your room?

ISABEL: Thank you.

CORNELIA: I've put you in the blue room. (*Intercepting a look from ISABEL to ARCHIBALD.*) Is something the matter? Have I done wrong?

ARCHIBALD: What it is my love, you've gone quite pale?

ISABEL: It's nothing. It's just…that it was father's room.

CORNELIA: It's the biggest bedroom in the house.

ARCHIBALD: I think Isabel means, her father passed away there.

CORNELIA: Well if no one was to sleep in rooms where people had died, we'd all be living in the streets.

ISABEL: Really, it doesn't matter. You're quite right.

CORNELIA: Oh no Maam, you must be right. It's your house. You are the mistress here.

CORNELIA and ARCHIBALD exit.

Scene 8

CORNELIA enters wielding a pair of garden shears. She and ISABEL are in the gardens at East Lynne.

ISABEL: Maybe I'll take a walk to meet Archibald on his way home.

CORNELIA: He'll be home when he's finished business for the day and no earlier.

ISABEL: Of course. I didn't mean for him to neglect anything –

CORNELIA: I cannot imagine what Peter thinks he's doing with these hedges. You can't expect to live in this sort of extravagant style and have the breadwinner endlessly at your elbow, you know. Unless you want us all to end up in the workhouse.

ISABEL: I'm sure I don't mean to be extravagant.

CORNELIA: He informed me he was cutting it in the shape of a chicken, if you please. Not out of my hedge you won't, I told him. The good Lord formed hens to make Sunday dinners, not to sit about pretending to be an aberration of a box hedge.

ISABEL: It's topiary.

CORNELIA: It's ridiculous. Speaking of which, what a perfect vanity of a hat.

ISABEL: I beg your pardon?

CORNELIA: At the turn in the lane. Barbara Hare coming to call. Again.

ISABEL: Oh. Oh yes. She's being very neighbourly.

CORNELIA: You'd have thought that family had enough scandal on its hands.

ISABEL: I don't understand.

CORNELIA: I keep forgetting what a newcomer you are to these parts. You don't know about Richard Hare?

ISABEL: No.

CORNELIA: Barbara's brother Richard is wanted for murder.

ISABEL: Oh no. For murder? How dreadful.

CORNELIA: I didn't mean to shock you. It was some years ago now. The shame of it made his mother an invalid. Which might explain why Miss Barbara is free to do as she pleases.

ISABEL: You've known the Hares a long time then?

CORNELIA: Barbara and Archibald grew up together. Mind, if she was my daughter she'd have been married off and living the other side of the county by now.

BARBARA enters.

So, Miss Barbara you are looking very fine.

BARBARA: Miss Cornelia. Lady Isabel.

ISABEL: How kind of you to call again, Miss Hare.

BARBARA: We may not be in high society, Lady Isabel, but we in West Lynne like to observe the niceties.

ISABEL: Oh of course.

BARBARA: I was hoping to see Mr Carlyle also.

CORNELIA: He'll be home when he's finished for the day.

BARBARA: How hard he works.

Beat.

ISABEL: And how is the harvest coming along?

BARBARA: I don't know I'm sure.

Silence.

Are you interested in farming, Lady Isabel?

ISABEL: No, not particularly. Music is my first love.

CORNELIA: I've no ear for music. None at all.

BARBARA: It must have sad associations for you.

ISABEL: Sorry?

BARBARA: Weren't you at Mr Kane's concert in West Lynne the night your dear father passed on?

And here you are, back again.

ISABEL: Cornelia tells me you've lived here all your life?

BARBARA: Oh yes. Archibald – Mr Carlyle – and I grew up together.

CORNELIA: I remember whipping the pair of you for stealing apples from that very orchard over there.

BARBARA: It was Archibald's idea. I just followed him. You know how young girls are.

CORNELIA: Yes.

Beat.

BARBARA: He's late.

CORNELIA: He's been coming home earlier each day.

ISABEL: Will you take some refreshment, Miss Hare?

BARBARA: Oh no, thank you. It's not the hour for tea yet. Ah here he is!

ARCHIBALD enters.

ARCHIBALD: What a lovely picture you make! My dear.

He kisses ISABEL.

And Barbara too. Did you walk from home?

BARBARA: Oh yes. You know me, I love to walk.

ISABEL: I'm afraid I'm not up to much these days.

Look from CORNELIA.

ARCHIBALD: Cornelia, might one enquire your purpose with those?

CORNELIA: Topiary.

BARBARA: Topiary?

ARCHIBALD: Yes Barbara, Isabel had a charming idea for creating some wildfowl who would never fly away.

CORNELIA: Have you any notion how long it takes to grow a decent box hedge?

ISABEL: It was only an idea.

BARBARA: Peter wouldn't like that.

CORNELIA: You know him Miss Barbara, he's happier digging the kitchen garden than messing about with fancy ideas.

ARCHIBALD: Come now Cornelia, you know very well Peter would gladly grow peaches in winter and grapes in the spring if her Ladyship requested it. He worships the ground she walks on. As do I.

ISABEL: Oh Archibald.

ARCHIBALD: Are you tired my dear?

ISABEL: A little. I'm sorry.

CORNELIA: What it is to be blessed with a healthy constitution.

ARCHIBALD: Isabel is made of finer clay than us Cornelia. She needs to be handled delicately. Especially at the moment.

BARBARA: Are you unwell Lady Isabel?

ISABEL: Oh no. Please Archibald.

ARCHIBALD: No my dear, I can't contain our secret any longer. Isabel is going to make me a father. And the happiest man in the world.

CORNELIA: (*Relieved.*) Oh, I thought you'd lost a client.

BARBARA: I'm delighted for you.

ARCHIBALD: Thank you Barbara, I knew you would be. You'll stay and take a glass of wine to celebrate.

BARBARA: No, thank you. I must go. Home. Goodbye.

ARCHIBALD: Oh but you've only just come…

BARBARA: Mama will need me.

ARCHIBALD: Is she not well again?

BARBARA: She has some business matters she would like your advice upon.

ARCHIBALD: Really? Then I must come at once.

ISABEL: But you've only just come home.

ARCHIBALD: You must forgive me my dear. Mrs Hare is an old and dear friend. And being an invalid it is hard for her to get out.

ISABEL: Yes of course.

ARCHIBALD: I won't be long my dear.

ARCHIBALD kisses ISABEL.

Come along Barbara. Don't look so gloomy. Whatever the matter is, I will do my best to help.

BARBARA: Lady Isabel, Miss Cornelia.

ARCHIBALD and BARBARA exit.

ISABEL: Archibald is so kind.

CORNELIA: Yes. And foolish enough to forget to put in his invoice. I must make a note.

ISABEL: They seem a much respected family hereabouts despite…

CORNELIA: Oh yes with him a Justice and her an invalid. But then there's young Richard – wherever he is.

ISABEL: To have a son convicted of murder. Poor woman! And poor Miss Hare also.

CORNELIA: Oh I shouldn't worry about young Barbara. She always was a determined child.

ISABEL: What do you mean?

CORNELIA is about to say something but changes her mind.

CORNELIA: I better order Archibald's tea. He's bound to come back with an appetite.

ISABEL: Miss Hare must be a great comfort to her mother.

CORNELIA: It's my opinion Barbara Hare would be a greater comfort if she found herself a husband. Of her own. Now, if you'll excuse me, Lady Isabel, I've got work to do.

CORNELIA exits.

Scene 9

JOYCE enters to dress ISABEL's hair.

JOYCE: Excuse me milady?

ISABEL: Yes?

JOYCE: It's only me milady. Come to help you dress.

ISABEL: Thank you. Joyce?

JOYCE helps her dress her hair.

JOYCE: Yes milady?

ISABEL: I overheard you and Peter gossiping this morning.

JOYCE: Oh did you milady?

ISABEL: Yes I did. About Miss Hare giving me a bowl of poison. What did you mean by that?

JOYCE: Oh nothing. It was only a bit of nonsense milady.

ISABEL: Really? Do go on.

JOYCE: Well, folks here know she held a torch for Mr Carlyle once upon a time. It was thought they'd be a match one day.

ISABEL: Indeed?

JOYCE: But it never came to nothing. Did it? And anyways, it's my opinion she'd never have made him happy. Not like he is now milady. If you don't mind my saying so.

ISABEL: But poisoning...they seem such a respectable family to have bred two violent children.

JOYCE: I wouldn't like to say about that milady.

ISABEL: Why not Joyce?

JOYCE: I'm involved so to speak.

ISABEL: In what way?

JOYCE: No way in particular.

ISABEL: Joyce.

JOYCE: Oh very well, if you will know it, Richard Hare murdered my father.

ISABEL: Oh how awful for you.

JOYCE: It was. Worse for father of course.

ISABEL: What happened?

JOYCE: It was my sister's fault. Afy Hallijohn. She got ideas above her station. Still has for all I know.

ISABEL: Oh dear.

JOYCE: Yes. She got them from the library in West Lynne. Ideas. Romantic notions. Next thing we knew, she'd taken up with Richard Hare, the Justice's son. I ask you. She should have known her place. But she was always a flighty piece. Soon she had him wound round her little finger. He hadn't got much in the attic, if you know what I mean. (*She touches her head.*) Pardon me milady but it's the truth.

ISABEL: How did it come about that Richard Hare shot your father?

JOYCE: Well, on the Thursday father hears offensive gossip in West Lynne coupling their names, so he tells Afy no gentleman go in secret after poor girls and to put an end to it. Friday, he's dead. Shot on the floor and Richard Hare running away from the house with blood on his shoes.

ISABEL: What became of your sister, of Afy?

JOYCE: Well when the Magistrates put out that Richard Hare was wanted for murder, she disappeared. So did he. Neither of them been seen since. They just left their shame behind for the rest of us to carry.

ISABEL: It wasn't your fault.

JOYCE: Fault's got nothing to do with it, milady. We've been given our paths to tread in life and we step off of them into the undergrowth, there's bound to be trouble for all concerned.

ISABEL: Indeed. Thank you for telling me Joyce.

JOYCE: Will that be all milady?

ISABEL: Yes. Joyce?

JOYCE: Yes milady?

ISABEL: The matter of Miss Hare and her...hopes for my husband – it was widely known?

JOYCE: Oh yes. It was no secret. But that's an old story. You don't want to go concerning yourself about that.

JOYCE exits. ISABEL is alone.

Scene 10

JOYCE enters with the baby and settles ISABEL and the baby together on the couch, wrapping them round with a shawl.

JOYCE: Isn't she a little treasure?

ISABEL: She's beautiful. The most beautiful thing that ever happened to me. Isabel Lucy.

JOYCE: I'm just showing Wilson where everything is.

ISABEL: Don't worry, we'll be all right.

JOYCE: I think she'll make a good nurse for the baby. Mrs Hare wouldn't have recommended her so highly else.

ISABEL: Her nails are so small. Look at her little feet.

JOYCE: Yes. Two of them. Mind she doesn't get in a draught now.

ISABEL: She won't, will you Isabel my pet. There.

ISABEL is totally engrossed in the baby. JOYCE leaves her and moves to sit the other side of the stage. WILSON approaches.

JOYCE: Ssh. They'll both be asleep in seconds.

WILSON: (*Peeping at ISABEL.*) She doesn't look well does she? Mrs Hare said she had a terrible time.

JOYCE: She'll be all right once she gets her strength back. And with you now to help with the baby, Wilson.

The two maids sort, fold, or sew on ribbons to tiny baby clothes as they talk, keeping their voices low.

WILSON: Well there's one I know be happy to take her place at a moment's notice.

JOYCE: Nonsense.

WILSON: It is not. I'm the one had to bear the brunt of her bad temper this past year since you know who got married.

JOYCE: Keep your voice down.

WILSON: All West Lynne knows Miss Barbara was in love with him, as much now as ever.

JOYCE: Idle gossip.

WILSON: No smoke without fire I say.

JOYCE: Mr Carlyle never cared for her.

WILSON: Ah but I've seen different. I've been witness.

JOYCE: To what?

WILSON: Only him kissing her.

JOYCE: That's not true.

WILSON: Strike me down with a thunderbolt if I lie. That's when he gave her that locket and chain and it's never been off her neck since.

JOYCE: More fool her.

JOYCE creeps to look at ISABEL who appears to be asleep. She comes back reassured.

WILSON: That's not the end of it, not by a long road.

JOYCE: Wilson, I don't wish to hear any more.

WILSON: Not much you don't, like about the night before he went off to get married and there they were having a regular little love scene about putting a piece of his hair in that same locket. And then off he goes and Miss Barbara bold as brass lifts up her face all glowing to the moon and says he'll never know how much she loves him till she's his wife.

JOYCE: Very likely. And him just about to be married!

WILSON: Well Lady Isabel had rank and beauty, didn't she? Turned his head and he threw over Miss Barbara for a title. He'd have been better off with the Hares' money. Nobody cries like she did when she heard the awful news, without having had some expectation. Sounded like her heart was being torn in little pieces. Poor thing.

JOYCE: Poor foolish thing to care for a man who didn't love her back.

WILSON: Who's to say he didn't? Only last summer I came upon the two of them by the gate to The Grove and her in tears and him saying henceforth they could only be like brother and sister. 'Don't betray me to your wife,' she said.

JOYCE: I don't believe a word of it.

WILSON: She still steals down to the lane about the hour she knows he'll be passing and watches him in secret. That's what's making her so bad-tempered. I couldn't take any more of it.

JOYCE: Well you won't have to. This is a very happy household. And milady is not going to die.

WILSON: I hope not, for Miss Barbara'd not make a very kind stepmother you can be sure.

There is a groan and a cry from ISABEL.

ISABEL: Joyce!

JOYCE: Whatever is the matter! Milady what is it? Let me take the baby. (*Looking at ISABEL.*) She's in a fever. Fetch Mr Carlyle.

WILSON: D'you think she heard?

JOYCE: No she can't have done. Quickly!

WILSON leaves.

There now, it's all right. Everything's going to be all right.

ISABEL: If I die, promise you'll take care of Isabel. Promise you won't leave her.

JOYCE: You're not going to die.

ISABEL: Promise.

JOYCE: I promise. I promise.

ARCHIBALD enters at speed.

ARCHIBALD: Isabel dearest, calm yourself.

ISABEL: Archibald promise me. Promise me.

ARCHIBALD: What happened Joyce?

JOYCE: Milady was asleep, with the baby, and then she cried out.

ARCHIBALD: Take the child to the nursery.

JOYCE leaves.

Isabel, dearest one, you were dreaming. Oh calm now, you mustn't make yourself ill again.

ISABEL: Promise me you'll never marry her. On your life, promise me. If I die…

ARCHIBALD: You're not going to die.

ISABEL: You loved her before didn't you? And since? Tell me. Please tell me.

ARCHIBALD: Who are you talking about?

ISABEL: You know. Of her, of Barbara Hare.

ARCHIBALD: I don't know how you came about this ridiculous notion but I promise you I never loved her, before or since our marriage.

ISABEL: But she loved you?

ARCHIBALD: Believe me you have no cause nor ever will have to be jealous of Barbara Hare.

ARCHIBALD leaves.

Scene 11

ISABEL: As mother to Isabel and then later to little Archie, as wife to Archibald Carlyle, I found a contentment and safety I had never felt before. Lady Isabel Carlyle, wife and mother. In my home, in East Lynne. Man and wife. Mother and children. I found peace. I forgot her, the young Lady Isabel, gauche and vulnerable, as she danced with the handsome Captain who was kind to her and made her laugh so that she would not cry. Instead I played with my children, took care of my husband, secure and steady, in my home, in East Lynne.

Scene 12

ISABEL is dressed ready for a journey. CORNELIA is sewing.

ISABEL: I've just time to go up and take one last look at them.

CORNELIA: Oh I wouldn't. You know what children are. You'll only upset them.

ISABEL: I'll play one last game with them while Peter harnesses the horses. That can't hurt.

CORNELIA: They'll get all excited and it'll only end in tears. The amount of noise those two make.

ISABEL: Now that Archie's better I don't care how noisy he is. I couldn't bear lying awake hearing him coughing.

CORNELIA: You'd sleep better at night if you did more during the day. There.

ISABEL: You're so efficient Cornelia.

ARCHIBALD enters.

Archibald.

ARCHIBALD: All ready to go?

ISABEL: Just a few more moments.

ARCHIBALD: We don't want to miss our crossing now do we?

ISABEL: (*Playing for time.*) I'm concerned about Isabel's new pony. I hope it's the right thing. She seemed a little nervous. You won't force her?

CORNELIA: She's a very lucky little girl to have a pony.

ISABEL: I know she is but perhaps it would be better to wait until I am back home again before she learns…

ARCHIBALD: Don't worry so. The children are in safe hands. I promise I will let no harm come to them in your absence.

CORNELIA: It will do them good to stand on their own two feet.

ISABEL: They're only little!

CORNELIA: There's no corner too small for the devil.

ARCHIBALD: Cornelia, could you see if the hamper is all packed?

CORNELIA: I know it is.

ARCHIBALD: Please be so kind as to check once more. You know how journeys increase my appetite.

CORNELIA: It would be much more economical if Peter were to travel with milady. What of business while you're away?

ISABEL: Oh business!

CORNELIA: It's business that's paying for your jaunting to foreign parts.

ARCHIBALD: It's only Boulogne, Cornelia, and I shall be back within two days. My clerk can handle things till then.

ISABEL: I don't want to go.

ARCHIBALD: And within six weeks we shall have Isabel back with us, fully restored to health... The hamper, Cornelia?

CORNELIA exits.

ISABEL: France. It's so far away.

ARCHIBALD: It's what Doctor Martin has recommended. And there you shall go. Doctor's orders.

ISABEL: If the children were coming with me it would be different.

ARCHIBALD: We've been through all this. Do I or do I not know what's best for my wife and children?

ISABEL: They're my children too! How can I get better if I'm worrying about them?

ARCHIBALD: Then don't worry.

ISABEL: You didn't see them just now when I said goodbye. Archie's little hands grabbing the air, trying to hold onto me. Nurse had to pull him away, great tears running down his face, his arms out...

ARCHIBALD: He'll get over it. Children do.

ISABEL: Not Isabel. She turned her head away when I tried to kiss her. She pretends she doesn't care but I heard her sobbing after Nurse had pushed me from the room and shut the door. I don't want to go Archie. Please don't make me leave my children!

ARCHIBALD: Now don't become all agitated my dear. That won't do you any good.

ISABEL: Leaving them won't do me any good either!

ARCHIBALD: Not this again. Please, Isabel. It's been decided. It's better for them, better all round.

ISABEL: Why do you listen to Cornelia rather than me? She's only worried about the expense.

ARCHIBALD: It's just her way to be prudent.

ISABEL: Then why not let me stay here? That won't cost anything.

ARCHIBALD: Now you're being silly. We're talking of your health, Isabel. It's my responsibility as your husband to see you get better.

ISABEL: Oh why won't you listen to me! Please!

ARCHIBALD: Now calm down. Doctor Martin was right. You really do need a rest away from all this. You're making yourself ill.

ISABEL: Ill? It's Cornelia isn't it? She wants me out of here.

ARCHIBALD: You just leave me to deal with life here at East Lynne.

ISABEL: I want to stay with my children. I want to stay with you. I don't want to go away.

ARCHIBALD: Of course you do. Look, here's Peter with the carriage. Off we go. All set for the seaside.

ISABEL looks as if she's about to make a run for it.

ISABEL: Just one last goodbye?

ARCHIBALD: Better not. It's all settled. Don't look so gloomy my dear. I'm only sending you away for your own good, because I love you. You know that, don't you?

ISABEL: Yes. Yes, Archibald. Thank you.

Scene 13

Boulogne.

ISABEL is alone. She has been walking but is now evidently very tired. LEVISON enters, watches her and then speaks.

LEVISON: I think you have gone too far this time, Lady Isabel.

ISABEL: I beg your pardon?

LEVISON: You don't remember me. Captain Levison.

ISABEL: Oh yes. Yes I do.

LEVISON: But things have moved on since then. Now I must address you as Lady Isabel Carlyle. Though you haven't changed.

ISABEL: Oh I have.

LEVISON: How nice to see you again.

ISABEL: Yes.

LEVISON: May I have permission to call upon you at your lodgings?

ISABEL: Yes.

LEVISON moves away.

Scene 14

ISABEL moves to a café table. LEVISON joins her.

ISABEL: (*Laughing.*) You mustn't talk about your uncle like that.

LEVISON: Why not? It's perfectly true. He thinks that
by marrying a young bride somehow her youth will
transfer to him. He is just like an old gorilla beating his
chest. Every time I enter the gates of Levison Park I
fully expect to see him come swinging through the trees
to meet me.

ISABEL: What nonsense.

LEVISON: True. He never comes to meet me. I'm barred
from the house and the country.

ISABEL: I think you must have been reading Mr Darwin.

LEVISON: Don't let the new Lady Levison hear you say
that of me or I should be forced to live abroad dodging
creditors for ever. To have descended from a monkey,
oh no, it's just not…

ISABEL: Elevating?

LEVISON: That's the very word. What does she think she
looks like?

ISABEL: Who?

LEVISON: That old fright over there, by the patisserie.

ISABEL: She reminds me of Cornelia.

LEVISON: Now then, you are here for your health. What
do you think…German? Certainly not French.

ISABEL: Perhaps. Yes, let's say German. She has a callous
on her heel where her new shoes hurt her, seven
children and twenty-three grandchildren who are all…

LEVISON: Little angels every one.

ISABEL: They can't all be.

LEVISON: To her they are. She has a large heart.

ISABEL: To match her feet. And her father…

LEVISON: Herr Strudel.

ISABEL: Ran a bakery shop.

LEVISON: Several bakery shops.

ISABEL: Where she was very happy throughout her childhood, playing amongst the flour sacks.

LEVISON: Which is why whenever she comes to a new town, she always goes first to –

ISABEL /LEVISON: (*Together.*) The patisserie!

ISABEL: Oh, I'm hungry.

LEVISON: Again?

ISABEL: These days I am always hungry.

LEVISON: Well first you have to earn it. To the cliffs and back. I'll race you.

ISABEL: I can't run. I'm an old married woman.

LEVISON: Oh of course. I forgot. Hey garçon. Over here. A bathchair please for my mother here. I want to push her round the sights.

ISABEL: (*Laughing.*) Ssh. People are looking.

LEVISON: Let them. Are you ready then?

ISABEL: No!

LEVISON: Steady?

ISABEL: No!

LEVISON: Go!

Scene 15

ISABEL: Look, there he is, coming out of the customs house! Archibald! Over here!

ARCHIBALD enters.

ARCHIBALD: My dear. What is this? A transformation! You look wonderful!

ISABEL: I feel it.

ARCHIBALD: Almost well again.

ISABEL: And this is Captain Levison. I wrote you in one of my letters that he was here. Don't you remember?

ARCHIBALD: I don't but...

LEVISON: And I'm glad I was here, Mr Carlyle, for I don't mind telling you now, I was shocked to see how your wife looked. I felt it my duty to help her.

ARCHIBALD: Thank you for doing so. You seem to have worked a miracle, or something has.

LEVISON: Shall I see you tomorrow? There is to be a carnival in the streets.

ARCHIBALD: Oh I think that might prove a little tiring for Lady Isabel, don't you?

LEVISON: Only if music and jollity are tiring. Everyone comes out onto the streets, the grandmothers in black, the children all sparkling with excitement. There are bands...

ARCHIBALD: (*Interrupting.*) Sounds very gallic. I tell you what. We should be able to get a good view from our window. Isabel and I shall wave to you from a position of safety.

LEVISON: You don't know what you're missing.

ARCHIBALD: (*Cheerfully.*) Probably not.

LEVISON: (*Drawing him aside.*) There was just one thing. I wonder if I might ask a favour...

ARCHIBALD: Anything my dear fellow. Anything.

LEVISON brushes back his hair with his jewelled hand, a familiar gesture.

ISABEL looks from one to the other, the two faces on her coin. So different from each other. She unconsciously copies LEVISON's gesture. She realises for the first time how involved she is with him, now she sees him beside her dull husband.

LEVISON moves off.

LEVISON: Thanks. I'm sure it would help my cause.

ARCHIBALD: My pleasure.

LEVISON exits.

What a charming man.

ISABEL: Yes. Archibald?

ARCHIBALD: Your cheeks have such roses in them.

ISABEL: I really think I'm well enough to come home now.

ARCHIBALD: How fortunate he was here.

ISABEL: What were you talking about?

ARCHIBALD: Captain Levison asked me to have a word with his Uncle, Sir Peter, on his behalf. Seems a pity a chap like that should be exiled abroad for want of a little understanding.

ISABEL: Archibald, please, please will you promise me something?

ARCHIBALD: If I can.

ISABEL: No, just promise me.

ARCHIBALD: Go on, what is it?

ISABEL: Stay here with me.

ARCHIBALD: You goose, I can't. I have a business to run.

ISABEL: Then let me come home with you tomorrow.

ARCHIBALD: What's brought this on?

ISABEL: I miss you. I don't want to stop missing you. Please. I'm strong now.

ARCHIBALD: Then you must stay here and become stronger.

ISABEL: I won't. I need to come home.

ARCHIBALD: Isabel, a fortnight since I left a shadow of my wife and I return to find you glowing, firmly on the way to recovery. Now tell me, would I be doing my duty to take you away from that now?

ISABEL: Forget your duty. Just listen to me, please listen to me. Trust me. I'm your wife.

ARCHIBALD: Precisely.

ISABEL: Then save me. I must come with you. I must.

ARCHIBALD: What you must do is continue the treatment. Clearly you are not as well as you first appear.

ISABEL: I promise you I am well enough to come home.

ARCHIBALD: You let me be the judge of that. Anyway, I've paid for these rooms for six weeks, what would Cornelia say!

ARCHIBALD leaves.

LEVISON joins ISABEL.

Scene 16

They are walking in a graveyard overlooking the sea.

ISABEL: All these people who never returned home to England. 'In loving memory of Susanna Rose.' I wonder if her family ever come to see their mother's grave. There's such a feeling of 'forever' here.

LEVISON: Death is the only forever. You sound wistful.

ISABEL: Oh no. I'm... (*She censors.*) I'm full of energy.

LEVISON: Do you have regrets?

ISABEL: Not yet.

LEVISON: Really?

ISABEL: I think I'm too young.

LEVISON: That's something. Do you remember an evening like this that we all passed at Richmond?

ISABEL: Richmond.

LEVISON: Your father, Emma Vane, you and me and some others.

ISABEL: Yes I do. The two Miss Challoners were with us and you drove Emma home. I remember she was cross because you drove recklessly and nearly put her in the ditch.

LEVISON: I did it on purpose.

ISABEL: Oh dear. What had she done to you?

LEVISON: Put me in a rage. She pushed herself forward, knowing it was not her I wanted to take home.

ISABEL: Ah yes, Blanche Challoner.

LEVISON: Emma accused me of caring for someone more than Blanche. She was right, the cat.

ISABEL: (*Changing the subject.*) The mistakes of youth.

LEVISON: We both played our cards like fools.

ISABEL: Look at the lights on the harbour. Is that the mail boat do you think?

LEVISON: I don't know. I have to say something.

Silence.

I was such a fool not to see that if ever two creatures were formed to love each other, it was you and me.

ISABEL: Please, no.

LEVISON: The dead can't hear us Isabel.

ISABEL: No. Don't.

LEVISON: I must tell you. I should have told you then, but my debts, my lack of prospects made me keep silent. I crushed my hopes and allowed you to escape.

ISABEL: I won't hear this.

LEVISON: But you must. For years I've thought of you, pictured you, longed for you – but never like this. I never knew how much I loved you until I lost you to him. When I saw you on the quayside I thought I'd imagined you there, I wanted you so much.

ISABEL: You mustn't talk to me like this. If you have any respect for me, stop. Now.

LEVISON: In a moment. Give me just this one moment. It can't harm us now. We've chosen different paths and must keep to them. But it was my fault. I should have spoken then and not allowed you to throw yourself away on him. On Carlyle.

ISABEL: I married him of my own free will…

LEVISON: Did you?

ISABEL: And I have never regretted it. He's the best, the kindest of men. The best husband and father.

LEVISON: That's as maybe. But not for you. Tell me honestly, did you never, for one second, alone at night dream of what our child might be like?

ISABEL slaps LEVISON.

ISABEL: That was cruel. That was not love.

LEVISON: I'm sorry.

ISABEL: Now, leave me alone.

LEVISON: I'm sorry. I'm truly sorry. I never meant to say that. I'll never mention what has passed between us again.

ISABEL: Nothing has passed between us Captain Levison. Nor ever will.

LEVISON: Isabel please.

ISABEL: Don't you understand? I can never see you alone again now. Ever. Nothing more. Good day.

LEVISON exits.

Scene 17

The drawing room at East Lynne. ISABEL looks discontentedly around her, sighs. CORNELIA enters carrying a pile of mending.

ISABEL: Oh Cornelia, is Archibald home yet?

CORNELIA: I hope not. He'd be neglecting his business if he was.

ISABEL: I suppose so. I wouldn't want him to do that.

CORNELIA: I should think not. After what that jaunting about on the continent must have cost.

ISABEL: I did return early.

CORNELIA: The English sea would have been quite good enough for me. Not that I'm ever ill, thank the Lord. But then I keep busy. That's the secret.

ISABEL: Joyce has taken the children out for a walk.

CORNELIA: Well there's this mending to be done. Nothing changes.

ISABEL: No. It's so hot in here.

CORNELIA: What are you doing?

ISABEL: Just trying to get some air. It's quite quite still. Not a leaf moving. In France the ocean breeze…

CORNELIA: I've ordered mutton for dinner.

ISABEL: Oh good.

ARCHIBALD enters.

Archibald!

ARCHIBALD: Hello dear.

Much as usual.

He picks up the paper.

Yours?

ISABEL: It's so hot.

ARCHIBALD: Good for the hay.

ISABEL: Oh, I wasn't complaining.

CORNELIA: I should think not. Dinner in half an hour Archibald.

ARCHIBALD: Good good.

CORNELIA exits.

ISABEL: I was thinking maybe of taking the children to the seaside.

ARCHIBALD: You've only just come from the seaside.

ISABEL: But they'd love the waves and perhaps they could learn to swim.

ARCHIBALD: Sounds a bit dangerous. Specially for Isabel.

ISABEL: Less dangerous than drowning, surely.

ARCHIBALD: They're happy enough here.

ISABEL: It was only an idea. What's happening in the world?

ARCHIBALD: Oh nothing much. The usual sort of thing. Nothing for you to worry about.

ISABEL: You know, in France the children have a custom…

BARBARA enters.

ARCHIBALD: Barbara. How nice.

BARBARA: Forgive me for coming straight in, Mr Carlyle. Lady Isabel. I trust you are still feeling well?

ISABEL: Oh yes. I'm full of energy now.

ARCHIBALD: Is everything all right?

BARBARA: Oh yes. I just came about about a business matter. For my mother.

BARBARA signals to ARCHIBALD she has something of great importance to tell him.

ISABEL: And how is dear Mrs Hare?

BARBARA: She says to thank you for the raspberry jelly. How well you know her little delights.

ARCHIBALD: My pleasure.

ISABEL: And Justice Hare, he's well?

BARBARA: Fine. How is that wicked pony? Has Isabel fallen off again?

ISABEL: Fallen? You never told me.

ARCHIBALD: You weren't here.

BARBARA: She didn't hurt herself. I put her straight back on and she soon cheered up. That's the way I learned.

ARCHIBALD: I remember. Blackie wasn't it?

BARBARA: Blackie. He was such a bolter. You know this pony reminds me of him. Wilful.

ARCHIBALD: Not with you in charge Barbara.

ISABEL: Isabel never told me about it.

ARCHIBALD: Why should she?

ISABEL: I am her mother.

ARCHIBALD: You weren't here.

ISABEL: But if she was frightened…

ARCHIBALD: Nonsense. She was fine, wasn't she?

BARBARA: I told her. She just needs to let the creature know who's in control. And I have the very thing.

BARBARA brandishes a child's riding crop.

ISABEL: Oh Miss Hare, you shouldn't have.

BARBARA: It was just lying about in the attic.

ARCHIBALD: Thank you. How very kind.

ISABEL: Well shall I leave you to your business?

BARBARA: Oh no. Really, it's of no matter.

BARBARA signals to ARCHIBALD to the contrary.

ARCHIBALD: I'll walk you home.

BARBARA: That would be kind.

WILSON enters.

WILSON: There's a gentleman to see you sir.

ARCHIBALD: A gentleman? Oh my good heavens yes. It clean escaped my mind. Show him in Wilson.

ISABEL: What gentleman Archibald?

LEVISON enters.

ARCHIBALD: Captain Levison. Welcome. Welcome to my home.

LEVISON: Mr Carlyle. Lady Isabel.

ISABEL: You?

ARCHIBALD: And may I introduce Miss Barbara Hare? A friend and neighbour. Captain Levison.

LEVISON: Enchanted, Miss Hare.

ARCHIBALD: This was the gentleman who was so kind to Lady Isabel and took care of her in Boulogne. Wasn't he Isabel?

ISABEL: Yes indeed. Archibald…

ARCHIBALD: And I must ask you to do the same again for a few moments while I see Miss Hare to her door. Wilson, tell Miss Cornelia there will be an extra person to dine. Come along Barbara.

WILSON exits.

Captain Levison, make yourself at home.

ARCHIBALD and BARBARA move off.

Scene 15

A montage scene of voices. LEVISON sits in a chair. The others are placed round the edge of the acting area, seen but not onstage.

ISABEL is central. As the scene progresses and LEVISON's insinuations and the evidence the others offer build, ISABEL becomes more distressed and less in control.

LEVISON: Who is this Barbara Hare who is here all the time?

ISABEL: I am here. In my house. In East Lynne. With my children and my husband. The summer is one to be talked about for years. So hot. So still.

LEVISON: Why is Barbara Hare here yet again?

ISABEL: She is visiting. A friend. A neighbour.

ARCHIBALD: Just a matter of business.

LEVISON: What sort of business?

ISABEL: I am Lady Isabel Carlyle. Wife. Mother. This is my house. My home.

BARBARA: Mr Carlyle, could I speak with you a moment? Archibald?

ISABEL: Let's take the children for a walk. In the shade, under the trees.

LEVISON: May I come too?

ISABEL: Of course.

WILSON: Miss Hare is in the study to see you.

ARCHIBALD: Just a matter of business.

BARBARA: Do you think he heard anything?

ARCHIBALD: Barbara my dear.

LEVISON: He walked her home again?

ISABEL: Never a day passes it seems without her being here and Archibald always ready.

WILSON: Well there's one who would fill her shoes readily if her ladyship should die.

BARBARA: I must speak with you.

LEVISON: She comes here often.

ISABEL: My husband is an honourable man.

WILSON: Miss Hare to see you in the study sir.

LEVISON: I don't want to see you hurt.

ISABEL: A neighbour.

ARCHIBALD: Barbara my dear.

BARBARA: Archibald.

ISABEL: An old friend of the family.

BARBARA: On business…for my mother.

WILSON: She always loved him. The whole town knows it.

ISABEL: Wasn't that Miss Hare at the door just now?

WILSON: She wanted Mr Carlyle Maam. She's gone away.

LEVISON: She'll be back.

ARCHIBALD: I shan't be long.

LEVISON: Courage my dear.

ARCHIBALD: Working late.

BARBARA: Is Mr Carlyle at home?

ARCHIBALD: At the office.

WILSON: Known him since childhood.

BARBARA: I can't thank you enough.

ISABEL: Enough.

WILSON: Always loved him.

LEVISON: Courage.

ISABEL: That is quite enough!

The other characters move off, except WILSON.

That will be all, Wilson.

WILSON exits.

Scene 19

ISABEL's bedroom. She is dressing. ARCHIBALD enters.

ISABEL: Can you help me with the clasp?

ARCHIBALD: Your mother's cross.

ISABEL: When we first met I was wearing this. Do you remember?

ARCHIBALD: (*Lying.*) Yes of course.

ISABEL: You are leaving it late to change. The carriage will be here directly.

ARCHIBALD: I'm afraid you're going to have to make my apologies to the Jeffersons.

ISABEL: What do you mean?

ARCHIBALD: I can't come with you to the party tonight.

ISABEL: But you must!

ARCHIBALD: Isabel, when I say I can't, I can't.

ISABEL: What shall I give as your excuse?

ARCHIBALD: It's a matter of business.

ISABEL: Ah business. That.

ARCHIBALD: Business keeps you in new frocks my dear.

ISABEL: It's old.

ARCHIBALD: Well it doesn't look it. Neither of you do. As soon as I've had a hasty dinner here I must go back to the office.

ISABEL: But you never go to the office in the evening.

ARCHIBALD: Tonight I must.

ISABEL: Very well. Go.

ARCHIBALD: Don't look at me like that.

ISABEL: Then tell me what the business is.

ARCHIBALD: I can't tell you.

ISABEL: Have a good evening then.

ARCHIBALD: (*Refusing to have an argument.*) And you too.

ARCHIBALD exits.

Scene 20

ISABEL: I leave the party early. I cannot be still. Only imagine. The air heavy with secrets. Archibald and Barbara. Barbara and Archibald. I have to get home.

LEVISON enters.

LEVISON: Lady Isabel! It's me.

ISABEL: Francis?

LEVISON: Out walking, in the moonlight.

ISABEL: Francis?

LEVISON: Look Isabel, look.

ARCHIBALD and BARBARA enter and stand together, deep in conversation. He comforts her.

ISABEL: And there in the grove, silvered by the moon, arms entwined, heads close…my husband and Barbara Hare!

ARCHIBALD and BARBARA exit separately. ISABEL cries out.

No! No!

LEVISON catches her as she falls.

LEVISON: Yes, it's true. I told you. He doesn't love you. I kept telling you. Why wouldn't you listen to me, my love? Hush now, it's all right, I'm here. I'll hold you. I'll love you. For ever and ever. You're safe now, with me. Come with me. Yes, that's it.

He is kissing her, stroking her, as she cries with hurt and anger.

How could he do that, how could he do that to you? There, where anyone could pass and see. How could he shame you so? Don't cry. I'll love you. I'll love you as he never has. You were made for me. And I for you. I'll never let you go.

ISABEL: I must go home.

LEVISON: Where they all know?

ISABEL: How could they?

LEVISON: You've heard the servants. The old affair started up again. How they must have enjoyed the scandal.

ISABEL: No. Stop it!

LEVISON: He doesn't love you. I do. Come with me. Now.

ISABEL: I must have time.

LEVISON: I'll wait for you tonight. Then I'll be gone.

LEVISON exits.

Scene 21

ISABEL is sitting in her bedroom, waiting.

ARCHIBALD enters and starts to take his outer clothes off ready for bed.

ARCHIBALD: My dear. Still up? A good party?

ISABEL: Fine.

ARCHIBALD: You made my excuses?

ISABEL: Yes.

ARCHIBALD: I was sorry to have missed it.

ISABEL: Were you?

ARCHIBALD: You foolish child still to be cross with me for not going with you. I told you, it was not my fault.

ISABEL: And your business went well?

ARCHIBALD: Oh, it wouldn't interest you. It was very dull. I must go to bed. I am dead asleep on my feet. Don't sit up too late.

ARCHIBALD starts to leave.

ISABEL: Too late.

ARCHIBALD: What?

ISABEL: Nothing.

ARCHIBALD exits.

ISABEL stands. She hears something.

'Mama'?

I go to their room. I look at them sleeping. Breath like hay. I kiss their necks, the scent damp and sweet. Archie mutters, turns over. Isabel sucks her finger, a graze on her elbow where she fell from the tree. I won't see it heal. How long before they hear the servants chatter, before they see them together. Poor Mama. I won't be pitied! Not by them! Moonlight through the curtains touches the hobby horse leaning in a corner, glass eyes glinting. He will wait only so long. And then he too will be gone. My darlings, it's not you I'm leaving. Oh God help me. God forgive me. I have no choice. The door shuts. Running silent to the carriage. A cloud across the moon. I forgot to cover Isabel up. A voice from the carriage. Francis calling: 'I love you. Always. Come. Now.' And I went.

Interval.

ACT TWO

Scene 1

ISABEL is sitting with a copy of East Lynne *on her lap. She reads.*

ISABEL: 'How fared it with Lady Isabel? Just as might be expected when a high principled gentlewoman falls from her pedestal. The very hour of her departure she awoke to what she had done and a lively remorse, a never dying anguish took possession of her soul forever. Oh reader believe me, lady, wife, mother, should you ever be tempted to abandon your home, so will you awaken. Whatever trials may be the lot of your married life, though they may appear to your crushed spirit as beyond the endurance of woman to bear, fall down upon your knees and pray to be enabled to bear them, pray for patience, pray for strength to resist the demon that would urge you to escape, rather than forfeit your fair name and your good conscience, for be assured that the alternative, if you rush on to it, will be found far worse than death.'

Thus wrote Mrs Henry Wood in her novel *East Lynne*. Love, jealousy, passion, what did she know of these? She was taught that feelings are dangerous. For every impure thought a flame flickers in hell's bonfire, waiting. Your duty is to honour and obey your husband, punish your children as you were punished, frighten your readers as you were frightened. Your duty is to keep control. So that when you die as you surely must, you will go to heaven with the angels.

ISABEL puts down the novel.

'How fared it with Lady Isabel?' Weary. We never stayed long in one place. Always moving, as if another country, another town would bring back the laughter between us, which had stopped almost as I stepped into the carriage that night outside East Lynne. Francis was a changed person once he had won what he coveted. An old story. I wanted to rest, to stay in one place, to recognise faces in the street. But no, always another border to cross, with me dragging behind, an encumbrance. Finally we stopped, in Grenoble, the baby was due in a month. Whatever Francis must do, I came to rest. To wait.

LEVISON enters and sits at a table where breakfast is laid. Two letters are on the table. He opens them then hides one under the tray as ISABEL moves to him.

ISABEL: Good morning.

LEVISON: Good morning.

ISABEL: Has it come?

LEVISON: What?

ISABEL: News of my divorce.

LEVISON: Not yet.

ISABEL: Isn't your letter from the solicitors?

LEVISON: Here, read it for yourself. I must pack. Pierre!

ISABEL: Where are you going?

LEVISON: To England of course. Pierre! To claim my title. Read it. You can call me Sir Francis from now on. Good old uncle Peter. That wasp of a wife of his must be livid he never managed to sire an heir before he died.

ISABEL: What about your child? Doesn't it deserve a name?

LEVISON: I can't marry you until you're divorced now can I?

ISABEL: But the decree is due any day.

LEVISON: And I'll be back any day.

ISABEL: Please don't go. The solicitors say that they can handle things.

LEVISON: I've been waiting for this all my life. Now I'm going home to claim what's mine.

ISABEL: What if the weather's bad and you cannot get a crossing back?

LEVISON: Do stop worrying. I can't control the weather just for your convenience.

ISABEL falls to her knees.

ISABEL: I'm talking about your child. A whole life, never to hold its head up. Born in sin it will have no place in the world. You know that. It's not for me I'm begging you, Francis. Think of the child. None of this is its doing. Please.

LEVISON: Isabel get up. You'll make yourself ill and what good will that do the child? Hm? Trust me. I have to go and I will be back and there's an end of it.

LEVISON kisses her quickly and exits.

Scene 2

ISABEL takes the letter from beneath the tray and reads it.

ISABEL: Not quite the end. Not quite. Every birth is a miracle. Each time quite different and none the less wonderful for that. I hadn't thought it possible to let another child into my heart. Holding the shawled baby I ached for Isabel and Archie. How they would have loved to have seen him, to have stroked his ears and his soft downy head. It wasn't his fault. Poor helpless little bundle.

At my window, the snow falling white and cold on foreign mountains, I admired him alone, wondering. And remembered my lost children.

LEVISON enters.

LEVISON: Isabel my dear. I'm so sorry.

He goes to kiss her. She moves away.

ISABEL: Why, did you forget to wipe your boots?

LEVISON: I beg your pardon?

ISABEL: And you should.

LEVISON: I was delayed by one thing after another but the moment I could come I did.

ISABEL: I see.

LEVISON: You look well. Where is he then? Does he resemble me?

ISABEL: I hope not, in any way.

LEVISON: Come now. I'm not that bad.

ISABEL: Why have you come here now?

LEVISON: To see you. To make sure you're are all right.

ISABEL: And then?

LEVISON: You sound so hard.

ISABEL: I have become practical.

LEVISON: Indeed?

ISABEL: When you left in July you said you would return before the baby was born.

LEVISON: And I tried to.

ISABEL: No you didn't. I found this letter amongst your things after you left.

LEVISON: I can explain.

ISABEL: Can you? You were able to marry me then and you deliberately lied that you intended to. Why?

LEVISON: You were in no state to listen to reason.

ISABEL: It was unreasonable to expect to become your wife?

LEVISON: Of course not. Then. But you must see how it is now. You come from a noble family yourself. In my position there is not only myself to think of. I wanted to do the right thing all round.

ISABEL: How would it have been wrong to marry me?

LEVISON: You and I know it isn't as easy as that. It would have been frowned on. If only divorce were not such a smear on one's name.

ISABEL: It is not on your name!

LEVISON: I can see you understand.

ISABEL: That you won't marry me because I am a divorced woman. You were happy enough before with the prospect.

LEVISON: I was thoughtless. Impetuous. One didn't think then of the consequences for one's family.

ISABEL: What about *my* family?

LEVISON: You left them.

ISABEL: For you, Francis, for you!

LEVISON: I think not.

ISABEL: (*Incredulous.*) Why then?

LEVISON: Didn't jealousy have something to do with it?

ISABEL: He turned from me.

LEVISON: So you believed.

ISABEL: What do you mean?

LEVISON: Well you'd never have left him otherwise, your dull dry lawyer. It was in your imagination Isabel.

ISABEL: What was?

LEVISON: Carlyle never cared for that woman; not in that way.

ISABEL: I don't believe you. I saw them together. You saw them. Whispering. You heard them.

LEVISON: Oh they had a secret right enough, but not of a romantic nature.

ISABEL: What then?

LEVISON: To do with her brother and the family scandal. He's wanted by the police.

ISABEL: Richard Hare?

LEVISON: Yes. Your husband was acting for Mrs Hare in the matter.

ISABEL: Hallijohn's murder.

LEVISON: Yes. Anyway, the girl was nothing but a messenger between her mother and your Mr Carlyle.

ISABEL: How do you know this?

LEVISON: I overheard some of their conversations.

ISABEL: Oh God. Nothing between them?

LEVISON: Only business. What else?

ISABEL: But you told me…

LEVISON: I wanted you. You believed me.

ISABEL: You lied to me, all that time?

LEVISON: All's fair in love and war. Is my room prepared?

ISABEL: Get out. I mean it.

LEVISON: So that's how it is? Well, perhaps you're right to turn me out. We'd have led each other a cat and dog life eh? Remember though, this is your doing, not mine. Here, take this for now. Later we'll fix an amount to be paid half yearly.

LEVISON holds out money.

ISABEL: You have ruined my life and you hand me money?

LEVISON: I won't have it said I let you starve.

ISABEL: Just go. Now.

LEVISON: What else will you live on?

ISABEL: My wits.

LEVISON: They won't get you far – you have nothing.

ISABEL: I have had nothing before.

LEVISON: Yes but now you have a past, Isabel.

ISABEL: Lady Isabel. I am still my father's daughter. You can't take that from me.

LEVISON: Goodbye then, Lady Isabel. It seems we are to part enemies.

ISABEL: No. Strangers.

LEVISON: Pity. A last word of advice, milady. If you want to work for a good family, you would do well to consider changing your name.

LEVISON exits.

ISABEL moves to the side of the stage and observes the next scene.

Scene 3

ARCHIBALD enters and looks at the breakfast table.

ARCHIBALD: Peter! Where's the paper? Peter…oh good morning Cornelia.

CORNELIA enters carrying the paper which she has obviously been reading.

I see you got there before me again. I do wish you would leave newspapers to me. There are no knitting patterns in *The Times*.

CORNELIA: I like to look at the obituary column.

ARCHIBALD: Well, have you had the satisfaction of seeing anyone of your acquaintance deceased this morning?

CORNELIA: Yes.

ARCHIBALD: You really have crumpled this up beyond recognition. Anyone I know?

CORNELIA: Yes. Somewhat.

ARCHIBALD: Oh my dear. Cornelia are you distressed?

CORNELIA: I rather think I am.

ARCHIBALD: Well where is it then? Obituaries. No. No. Ah. 'As the result of a train accident, at Cammere France, on the 18th inst. Isabel Mary, only child of William, late Earl of Mount Severn.' Isabel, dead?

CORNELIA: It's too terrible. And you didn't read the worst of it. 'Also her infant son.'

ARCHIBALD: Isabel Mary, only child… Isabel dead?

CORNELIA: Poor little thing. I never knew there was a baby. Oh dear.

CORNELIA cries.

I'm so sorry Archie. Maybe it's for the best.

ARCHIBALD: The best?

CORNELIA: I never knew there was a baby. Did you?

ARCHIBALD: Goddammit Cornelia! My wife is dead! Hold your tongue. Isabel is dead!

CORNELIA: Oh Archie I'm so sorry. My dear...

ARCHIBALD: Don't say any more Cornelia please.

CORNELIA: I do understand how you must...

ARCHIBALD: Would you be so kind as to ask Peter for some more tea. This has gone quite cold.

CORNELIA: The shame of it. The terrible shame. No amount of damages that man, Levison, has paid you can make up for this.

ARCHIBALD: The tea please Cornelia.

CORNELIA: What shall I tell the children?

ARCHIBALD: Tell them nothing.

CORNELIA: But she was their mother.

ARCHIBALD: She was as one dead the moment she left this house. Let her remain so. If you please, the hot water.

CORNELIA exits.

ARCHIBALD stands shocked until she returns.

CORNELIA: It's on its way.

ARCHIBALD: Thank you.

ARCHIBALD starts to leave.

CORNELIA: Where are you going?

ARCHIBALD: To the office. Business as usual.

CORNELIA: Business as usual.

CORNELIA exits.

Scene 4

ISABEL picks up the paper and reads the obituary.

ISABEL: 'As a result of a train accident, at Cammere France, on the 18th inst. Isabel Mary, only child of William, late Earl of Mount Severn. Also her infant son.'

But in a French hospital lay Madame Veen, splinted and scarred beyond recognition. Her back was broken, her face scarred, her hair streaked with silver.

I had wanted to die and this was a kind of death. The nurse enquired if I was finished with the paper. I said yes, quite finished.

Performer playing JOYCE enters with glasses, cape and bonnet which ISABEL puts on, transforming herself into Madame Veen.

Scene 5

AFY approaches ISABEL.

AFY: Good evening Madame Veen.

ISABEL: Good evening. I don't believe I know…

AFY: We haven't met but I'm companion to Mrs Latimer who's taken up with your Mrs Crosby. You're governess to her daughter, aren't you?

ISABEL: Yes. Well that is…

AFY: Is it true Miss Helena's to be married to that old Count von whatsisname?

ISABEL: She is engaged yes.

AFY: You'll be out of a job then, I suppose.

ISABEL: You seem to know a lot about me.

AFY: Well, it's a dreary hole isn't it. And where we're lodging not a soul speaks English. God's honest truth, I never thought I'd miss West Lynne, dull place that it is, but I do.

ISABEL: You come from West Lynne?

AFY: Yes, horrid place.

ISABEL: Why don't you like it there?

AFY: Because I don't.

ISABEL: Do you know East Lynne?

AFY: I ought to, my sister Joyce is head maid there.

ISABEL: Joyce?

AFY: Yes. Joyce Hallijohn. I'm Afy. Do you know her?

ISABEL: No. I… Some years ago I stayed in the area and spent a happy time there. And her name is distinctive.

AFY: And we all know why. You must have heard of my father's murder? Set the tongues wagging like a dog's tail that did, and never stopped since far as I'm concerned.

ISABEL: Do the Carlyles still live there? They were such a nice family.

AFY: Yes they do, but there have been some changes since then. I daresay you were there in the time of Lady Isabel?

ISABEL: Yes. She was Mr Carlyle's wife, wasn't she?

AFY: Nice wife she made him. You must have heard all about that, Madame Veen, unless you went about with your hands over your ears.

ISABEL: Perhaps I did. I forget.

AFY: She ran off with another man, left her children too. Unnatural if you ask me.

ISABEL: How are they?

AFY: Who?

ISABEL: The children.

AFY: They're all right, poor little things. Well, one of them's on the road to consumption to my mind, but Joyce denies it, gets in a temper if I say so.

ISABEL: Which one? Isabel?

AFY: Isabel?

ISABEL: The eldest child, Miss Isabel Carlyle.

AFY: There's no Isabel. Only Lucy.

ISABEL: No Isabel!

AFY: Wait a minute, I know why you got it wrong. She used to be called Isabel same as her mother, I remember Joyce telling me, but the night her mother left, Mr Carlyle gave orders she was to be called by her second name from then on. Lucy.

ISABEL: I see.

AFY: Couldn't bear to hear the name again, poor man. No, it's the boy that's ill. That's only my opinion mind.

ISABEL: Archie.

AFY: Fancy you remembering. You must have been awful fond of them.

ISABEL: I was.

AFY: Yes. He's as thin as a herring and he's got that look about him.

ISABEL: What look?

AFY: Joyce says his cheeks are bright like his mother's but I know different. Healthy folks don't look like that. Here, did you know the sister? Miss Corny?

ISABEL: I have seen her.

AFY: Constitution of a goods train. She was good to our Joyce though.

ISABEL: Is she still at East Lynne?

AFY: Joyce is – she promised Lady Isabel to stay with the children and she's one to keep her word.

ISABEL: And the sister?

AFY: Oh no, Miss Corny's gone. There'd have been blood flowing between her and Mrs Carlyle if she'd stayed.

ISABEL: What?

AFY: You only want one mistress in a house.

ISABEL: Mrs Carlyle?

AFY: Yes. Mr Carlyle's wife.

ISABEL: He married again?

AFY: Are you sure you feel all right?

ISABEL: It's just the heat. I have a slight fever. I didn't know he was married again.

AFY: Oh yes. I went to the wedding – must be a year and a half ago. She looked lovely. All West Lynne turned out to see her. She waited long enough to get him.

ISABEL: Not Barbara Hare?

AFY: Didn't come as a surprise to anyone else either. Though it was said that if Lady Isabel hadn't 'ave up and died, Mr Carlyle would never have married again. Still, there's a baby now. Lovely little boy, apple of his mother's eye. She worships the pair of them, him and Mr Carlyle. It's lovely really, a happy ending, isn't it?

ISABEL looks about to faint.

Here, get your head down. Can't have you fainting in a public gardens now, can we?

ISABEL: I'm all right.

AFY: Sure?

ISABEL: Thank you. Do you know, is she kind to the other children? Mrs Carlyle.

AFY: For all I know. They're mostly with the governess.

ISABEL: A governess?

AFY: I suppose he had to get someone to look after them. Mind she's leaving to get married, Joyce says.

ISABEL: Are you much at East Lynne?

AFY: No. Mrs Carlyle disapproves of me. She knows her brother Richard would have given his head to marry me.

ISABEL: Richard?

AFY: Yes, Richard Hare. Mind he was no great catch even before he went to the wrong. He had class but no brains. And those seedheads in West Lynne thought I ran off with him. After he murdered my own father! As if I would. Between you and me, I had another suitor. He was a handsome devil he was. And a gentleman. He had class and brains. Still.

ISABEL: Barbara Hare.

AFY: Just think, if Lady Isabel hadn't gone off like that, Barbara Hare wouldn't even be Mrs Carlyle now and I could go and visit my sister whenever I please. I expect we'll meet again.

ISABEL: Yes. Good night.

AFY exits.

Scene 6

MRS CROSBY enters.

MRS CROSBY: Madame Veen? Madame Veen? Could I have a word?

ISABEL: Yes, Mrs Crosby. I'm sorry I was having a rest.

MRS CROSBY: Your leg still pains you?

ISABEL: I must learn to live with it. Does Helena require…

MRS CROSBY: No no. Now she's engaged she's got no more need of learning.

ISABEL: Indeed. She's very happy.

MRS CROSBY: So are we. But I came to talk about you.

ISABEL: It's very kind but you mustn't worry about me.

MRS CROSBY: Oh I'm not. Not now.

ISABEL: Good.

MRS CROSBY: I was yesterday. I know the notice was rather sudden. Young love you know. But I've found a solution.

ISABEL: I'll find another position I'm sure.

MRS CROSBY: You don't need to. I've found the very one. My friend Mrs Latimer told me. Such a nice family, very well set up, a most desirable situation. And she says it's a beautiful place, East Lynne. You've been so good with my Helena, I think you'd be just the person those children are looking for. Don't you?

ISABEL: East Lynne. I'll…need some time to think it over.

MRS CROSBY: It's all right. It's all arranged. Positions like that are few and far between. They're waiting, Madame Veen.

MRS CROSBY exits.

Scene 7

ISABEL has just arrived in the drawing room at East Lynne. Her old home. She looks around. It is all wonderfully familiar. BARBARA enters.

BARBARA: Madame Veen. I am Mrs Carlyle. I trust you are refreshed after your journey?

ISABEL: Yes, thank you.

BARBARA: And you like your room?

ISABEL: Yes it will do fine, thank you.

BARBARA: Do sit down. Are you quite well?

ISABEL: It's just the travelling. I am normally very healthy.

BARBARA: Mrs Latimer spoke very highly of you. I do hope you'll be happy here. Have you lived much in England?

ISABEL: Once I did, yes.

BARBARA: And you lost your husband and children? Forgive me, I didn't mean to be so abrupt, Mrs Latimer did mention children didn't she?

ISABEL: Yes. I have lost them.

BARBARA: I can't imagine anything more awful. I couldn't bear to lose my baby. You must meet him. He's the most beautiful creature. But he will not be in your charge. You are aware that the other two are the children of Mr Carlyle's first wife.

ISABEL: And Mr Carlyle.

BARBARA: Yes, of course. Their position, particularly the girl's, is difficult as well as sad. Their mother left them.

ISABEL: I heard she was dead.

BARBARA: We don't speak of her to the children. Better not to remind them of the disgrace, though the shame will always taint them I'm afraid. Mr Carlyle wants them to forget her. Unfortunately she was the children's mother. There's nothing we can do about that except instil them with the strictest principles.

ISABEL: Do you have the children much with you?

BARBARA: I firmly believe a child ought never to hear anything but gentleness from a mother's lips, and this becomes impossible if she is very much with the child. Don't you agree?

ISABEL: Oh oh yes. Of course.

BARBARA: How many children did you have Madame Veen?

ISABEL: Two…and a baby. That died. Died an infant, I mean.

BARBARA: How tragic. What did they die of?

ISABEL: Of, of illness.

BARBARA: How sad. Forgive me asking these things but not having met you in person before. You are obviously a gentlewoman.

ISABEL: I was born and reared so, yes.

BARBARA: How dreadful to have fallen on hard times. Mr Latimer said your husband did not leave you well provided.

ISABEL: When I lost him I lost everything.

WILSON enters with the baby.

BARBARA: Ah here's my precious.

WILSON stares at ISABEL.

Has he been a good boy Wilson? Wilson!

WILSON: Oh yes Mrs Carlyle Maam. Good as gold.
Though he will keep kicking his covers off.

BARBARA: Naughty boy. Look Madame Veen. Isn't he
the most beautiful baby you ever saw?

ISABEL: Beautiful. Just like, he doesn't resemble you.

BARBARA: No, not by an eyelash. He's just like his father,
aren't you? Yes you are. Look at him laugh.

ISABEL: What's his name?

BARBARA: Arthur. Arthur Archibald. I had wanted
Archibald for his first name but it was already taken.
They aren't playing rough games too near the baby I
hope?

WILSON: Don't worry Maam. There's no misbehaving in
my nursery.

ARCHIBALD enters.

BARBARA: Why my dear, you're back so soon?

ARCHIBALD: I couldn't stay away.

BARBARA: Thank you Wilson. Wilson. You may go.

Taking a last look at ISABEL, WILSON exits.

How was Papa?

ARCHIBALD: Full of volume as always.

BARBARA: Did you ask him how Mama is?

ARCHIBALD: 'Full of nervous fidgets.' I quote. And how
is my fine son?

BARBARA: Far from sleep. But my dear, you must meet Madame Veen.

ARCHIBALD: Forgive me Madame. I hadn't noticed you, sitting so quietly in the corner there.

He puts out his hand, ISABEL has to shake it.

Do you have enough light?

ISABEL: Quite enough, thank you.

ARCHIBALD: I hope you'll be very happy in our home.

ISABEL: I'm sure I shall. Will you excuse me? I'd like to go to my room.

BARBARA: Of course.

BARBARA and ARCHIBALD exit.

Scene 8

ISABEL: I should never have come back. I will leave in the morning, after I've had just one glimpse of my children. I want to creep to their bedside – only to look at them breathing. But I'm afraid of frightening them if they wake and find a stranger leaning over them. I round the bend in the corridor and there, running towards me –

ISABEL opens the toy box and takes out a spinning top and a horse. They symbolise ARCHIE and LUCY respectively and ISABEL talks to them whilst she hears their voices from the side of the stage.

The following is a montage scene. ISABEL is alone on stage.

ARCHIE: Are you our new governess?

LUCY: The last one taught us music – can you play the piano? Mama wants us to keep up with it.

ISABEL: Mama?

LUCY: This is the schoolroom.

ISABEL: How you've grown.

LUCY: What?

ISABEL: It's a lovely room.

BARBARA: Discipline at all times.

ARCHIE: Do you want to watch us having our breakfast?

LUCY: Our bath?

ISABEL: I'd like that.

ARCHIE: Isn't she weird?

ISABEL: Aren't they wonderful?

BARBARA: It doesn't do to get too fond.

ARCHIE: Hate porridge.

ISABEL: Still.

BARBARA: Every scrap. Think of the poor and needy.
    Kind but firm.

ISABEL: My eyes. Her father's hair. How pale he looks.

ARCHIE: Aunt Cornelia wants us to grow up like him but
    Joyce says we still look like her.

LUCY: We always had breakfast with Papa in the old days.

ISABEL: Careful, don't lean out.

LUCY: Not since mamma came.

ISABEL: Oh don't go Isabel.

BARBARA: It doesn't do to get too fond.

ARCHIE: Her name's Lucy.

LUCY: Lucy.

BARBARA: Miss Lucy's a bit of a handful. It's in the blood.

ISABEL: I'm sorry?

LUCY: No one's called me Isabel since mama went away.

BARBARA: We all are. Such a shame. On both of them.

LUCY: She was kidnapped!

ARCHIE: A bad man stole her away in the night.

LUCY: I'm going to kill him if I find him.

ARCHIE: With a sword.

LUCY: Or a cutlass –

ARCHIE: She'd never have left us. Would she?

LUCY: Would she?

ISABEL: I expect your mama loved you very much.

BARBARA: It doesn't do to get too fond. It just doesn't do.

ISABEL: Don't cry, my pet.

ARCHIE: Got something in my eye.

LUCY: We must not love her any longer.

ARCHIE: We've been told.

ISABEL: You could love me.

LUCY: Anyway she's dead.

ARCHIE: Our Mama's dead.

ISABEL slams shut the toy box.

Scene 9

ISABEL is holding the top. BARBARA comes in with a shopping list.

BARBARA: Good housekeeping is at the heart of a happy family. That's what my mother would say. Cleanliness, Godliness and always pay the tradesmen on time. You look tired, Madame Veen.

ISABEL: I have been worried.

BARBARA: Oh dear, we can't have that. What about?

ISABEL: About Archie. His cough is so heavy in his chest. Much worse now it has come back. And especially at night time. If I were to stay with him, sleep in his room I am sure it would be a comfort to him.

BARBARA: Madame Veen, it is quite out of the question.

ISABEL: Please let me.

BARBARA: Certainly not. Whatever are you thinking of? There are servants for that. Now then, if you would be so kind as to see to these errands for me whilst Archie is with the doctor. I would go myself but the approach to Christmas is such a busy time for a wife and mother. Joyce will help you carry your parcels. Whatever is that you have there?

ISABEL: An old toy of Archie's. I found it hidden away.

BARBARA: That old thing? Why Madame, he stopped playing with that years ago.

ISABEL: He did? Well then I shall look for something else in the toy shop today instead.

BARBARA: Ah yes. I've been meaning to have a word with you about that. Please don't take this amiss but my husband and I would both rather you didn't keep giving presents to the children.

ISABEL: But it's Christmas!

BARBARA: Nevertheless. We worked out what you must have spent on them already and it is more than half your salary.

ISABEL: I have no one else to spend the money on. I love the children.

BARBARA: I'm sure you do, but you have yourself to think of. Your old age.

ISABEL: I'm not concerned about that.

BARBARA: Please, be so kind as to take the hint Madame and do not oblige me to forbid your generosity. It is very kind of you, very good, but if you do not think of yourself, we must think for you.

ISABEL has no option. BARBARA exits.

Scene 10

ISABEL joins CORNELIA who hands her a basket containing Christmas wrapped boxes. CORNELIA is also carrying a basket. They are outside in the streets of West Lynne.

CORNELIA: My goodness what a crush. He almost pushed me under that carriage. (*Angry.*) And a merry Christmas to you too! Has the world gone mad?

ISABEL: I love Christmas. That is, I used to.

CORNELIA: An excuse to spend large amounts of money on utterly useless objects. I have brought Archibald four pairs of woollen socks and two linen handkerchiefs as I have always done.

ISABEL: What of surprise?

CORNELIA: Life is plenty full of surprises without courting trouble, Madame. Why only this morning I found a beetle in a sack of flour. As I am about to tell Mr Jiffin, if I had wanted a beetle I would have purchased a sack labelled 'flour and beetle'. I did not. I do not. I have the offending insect in my reticule, would you care to see it?

ISABEL: I have quite a few more errands for Mrs Carlyle before collecting Archie.

CORNELIA: I'll come with you. Once I have dealt with the matter of the beetle. Meet me here.

ISABEL: I don't want to be late for Archie.

CORNELIA: Get a move on then. Oh good Lord, how it snows. Excuse me. That was my foot.

ISABEL: But Miss Carlyle…

CORNELIA exits. ISABEL checks her list and turns to see FRANCIS LEVISON coming towards her. ISABEL gasps and freezes to the spot. LEVISON stands aside and raises his hat to her.

LEVISON: Excuse me Maam. Nasty weather. Allow me.

LEVISON nods and exits. ISABEL is left standing in shock.

ISABEL: Francis? Here? Oh my dear God.

CORNELIA bustles up.

CORNELIA: I'm not waiting twenty minutes to return a beetle. You'd think people were afraid they might die of hunger over Christmas! Have you purchased the lace then? Madame Veen? I thought you were in a hurry. You'd better give me the list. Now then, crystallised fruits!? Why not crystallised sovereigns and be done with it? Well, come along then.

JOYCE enters in a state of high excitement.

JOYCE: Oh Miss Carlyle. You'll never guess what's come about!

CORNELIA: So why don't you tell me?

JOYCE: He's here. In West Lynne. Bold as brass Miss Carlyle. I couldn't believe my eyes. But it was him, I swear it.

CORNELIA: Joyce, you are not a headless chicken. Kindly stop talking in circles. Who is here?

JOYCE: Him. Sir Francis Levison.

CORNELIA: Don't be ridiculous. He'd never dare show his face here again. After the shame he wrought on my family!

JOYCE: But it's true. He's here.

CORNELIA: Come along. Mr Carlyle must be informed at once. He'll put a stop to this. Madame Veen!

CORNELIA and JOYCE exit.

ISABEL: Everyone is here now. All the characters in my drama assembled. And I can only stand and watch as we roll towards the edge. The sun shines clear through a blue winter sky, the lawns crisp with frosted snow, the horses' hooves kick up gravel as the doctor leaves. My son is ill and still the sun shines.

Scene 11

ISABEL is watching out of the window as ARCHIBALD enters.

ARCHIBALD: Ah, Madame Veen.

ISABEL: Yes, Mr Carlyle?

ARCHIBALD: The doctor has gone?

ISABEL: Yes, he just drove away.

Silence.

He saw Archie?

ARCHIBALD: Yes.

Silence.

ISABEL: Forgive me sir, but what did he say?

ARCHIBALD: What did he say? Yes.

ISABEL: Yes?

ARCHIBALD: He was concerned.

ISABEL: I'll go to him.

ISABEL goes to leave and almost collides with JOYCE who is running across the room with a tray of syrup, spoon, glass, jug of water. Her apron has blood on it.

ARCHIBALD: What is it?

JOYCE: I just needed to get him some syrup sir, he does like it.

ARCHIBALD: Of course. Whatever he wants.

ISABEL: How is he?

JOYCE: He's all right now.

ISABEL: But your apron!

JOYCE: He coughs so hard. He's quiet now.

ISABEL: He's not alone?

JOYCE: No, Mrs Carlyle is with him.

ARCHIBALD: You should have called me, I don't want her to be upset. Not now.

ISABEL: Let me go. I know how to soothe him.

JOYCE: His poor little chest.

ARCHIBALD: No Madame Veen. I think it best not to crowd the boy. You sit with him Joyce.

ISABEL: Let me sir, please.

ARCHIBALD: There's nothing you can do Madame. What are you standing there for Joyce? Go to him.

JOYCE leaves.

ISABEL: He likes me to tell him stories. About when he was a baby.

ARCHIBALD: A baby?

ISABEL: I make them up.

ARCHIBALD: All the stories in the world won't help him now, Madame. The doctor's news was not good. We must be very brave. For Archie's sake, and for Mrs Carlyle. This is a difficult time for her.

ISABEL: Why? She's not his mother!

ARCHIBALD: Madame Veen, you forget yourself.

ISABEL: I'm sorry sir but I'm so fond…

ARCHIBALD: Enough goddammit! Have I not enough to bear?!

ISABEL: I'm sorry, Mr Carlyle.

ARCHIBALD: So am I, Madame Veen, so am I. I didn't mean to speak harshly. You might as well know, the whole town will be buzzing with it by now. Sir Francis Levison was arrested this morning for murder.

ISABEL: For murder?

ARCHIBALD: Of Hallijohn. Dear God, all those years, the anguish he caused the Hare family. Richard hunted into exile. The suffering he caused Barbara and her mother. God forgive me, I never thought I'd be glad to see a man hang.

ISABEL: Dear God.

ARCHIBALD: And then what he did to my wife!

ISABEL: Your wife?

ARCHIBALD: Isabel. Lady Isabel. He ruined her life. I trusted him, I invited him into my house. I thought he was a gentleman! At least she has been spared this. Poor woman.

ISABEL: You pity her?

ARCHIBALD: I loved her. She was so beautiful. When I look at Archie I see her again, my wife. My beautiful boy. I don't know what I shall do without him.

JOYCE runs in.

JOYCE: Could you come, he's calling for you?

ISABEL: Of course.

JOYCE: Sir.

ARCHIBALD: I'll come at once.

JOYCE and ARCHIBALD exit, leaving ISABEL alone. She waits.

Scene 12

It is night. Dawn approaches. WILSON enters from ARCHIE's room offstage.

ISABEL: He's asleep again?

WILSON: I don't like the look of him.

ISABEL: Dr Martin said he still had time – a week or so.

WILSON: Martin's an old man. He likes to keep his customers happy.

ISABEL: His breathing's so harsh.

WILSON: They've been wondering, in the kitchens, which of his grandpas he'll be laid next to. Lord Mount Severn or old Mr Carlyle. Be different if she'd died at home. He'd have gone in the vault next to her. Her Ladyship, you know.

Silence.

I wonder what he's thinking about now in Lynneborough jail. That Sir Francis Levison. I'll wager several trainfuls will go from West Lynne to see him hang. I always knew he was a bad man. And that Afy Hallijohn boasting of her two fine lovers – Richard Hare as weak as water and now Levison, a murderer. Any fool could see he was no good. But then she keeps her brains under her petticoats.

Silence.

Well, I'll be off to my bed. I'll tell Joyce to come up shall I Madame?

ISABEL nods.

And his father. Best they all come quick.

WILSON exits.

ISABEL cries out.

ISABEL: No! No!

ISABEL wrenches off her bonnet and glasses in her distress. She weeps. She does not hear JOYCE come in. JOYCE stands looking at her in shock, seeing a ghost.

JOYCE: Oh my God! May God forgive me, you've come back to take him. Forgive us our trespasses as we forgive them... Milady is it really you?

ISABEL: Don't betray me. I had to see my children again.

JOYCE: Dear Father in heaven. You're supposed to be dead. They said you had died. In France.

ISABEL: I survived.

JOYCE: You shouldn't be here. What if she comes, or Mr Archibald? No, you shouldn't be here milady. This is wrong.

ISABEL: I couldn't help it. I heard he was ill.

JOYCE: No one else knows?

ISABEL: No one.

JOYCE: I have thought. I've seen it but I thought it was my imagination.

ISABEL: Joyce, I never knew he had done that, that he killed your father. Believe me, if I had known...

JOYCE: It's all right milady, I know.

ISABEL: He called for you.

JOYCE exits.

ISABEL waits.

JOYCE enters.

JOYCE: Merciful heaven, it's over.

ISABEL: No. It's too soon. It can't be.

JOYCE: He's gone over now. He'll be all right now.

ISABEL: No! Archie. Darling.

ISABEL tries to run to ARCHIE. JOYCE holds her.

JOYCE: Hush milady. Leave him now. He's gone. Don't let them hear you. Be careful, please.

ISABEL: Let me have just one moment. He never knew.

JOYCE: I must tell his father.

ISABEL: Yes.

ISABEL goes to the window.

Someone's ringing the tradesman's bell. The early
sun is shining through the trees. A robin pulls at a
worm. Archie's left his shoe on the wet grass beside
the old battered hobby horse. Its eyes glint in the light.
No more. Day following endless day. How can I live
through all those hours, all those mornings without him?
Every minute, every second knowing he will never ever
wake up and call out again. I cannot bear this, Joyce.

JOYCE: You have to milady.

ISABEL: Yes I know. I know I do.

JOYCE exits.

Scene 13

ISABEL: Spring will not come again to East Lynne. A
sudden sharp breeze scurries across the ice-trapped
river, lifts a flurry of snow on a chase through the tree
trunks along the lane where Barbara Hare watched and
waited. Darting into a drift the wind urges the snow on
past The Grove and The Grange, past the damp cottage
where Afy Hallijohn's father died, past the townhouses
with their wreathes spotted with blood red berries,
along the busy high street twinkling with Christmas
tinsel and finally ducks under the lytch gate, and comes
to rest in the churchyard. And see there, beneath the
great yews, their branches heavy iced with snow, the
grave of Lady Isabel Vane. No remembrance, just the
initials. It is a cold place. But not as cold as the hearts of
those who dwell in East Lynne.

At Windsor Victoria spends her first Christmas without
Albert and the royal household all wear mourning.
In the rural village of Upper Norwood, Mrs Henry
Wood lays down her pen, shuffles the pages of her
novel together, and goes with her husband and family
to church. A Christian woman in a Christian country,

smiling at her neighbours, celebrating the spirit of forgiveness and redemption.

It is not so for me. I stand then as now, outside the walls of her church, her life, her judgement. And the snow falls on me and women like me. And we feel the cold. Then as now.